THE RISE AND FALL OF THE
BERLIN WALL

THE RISE AND FALL OF THE
BERLIN WALL

R.G. Grant

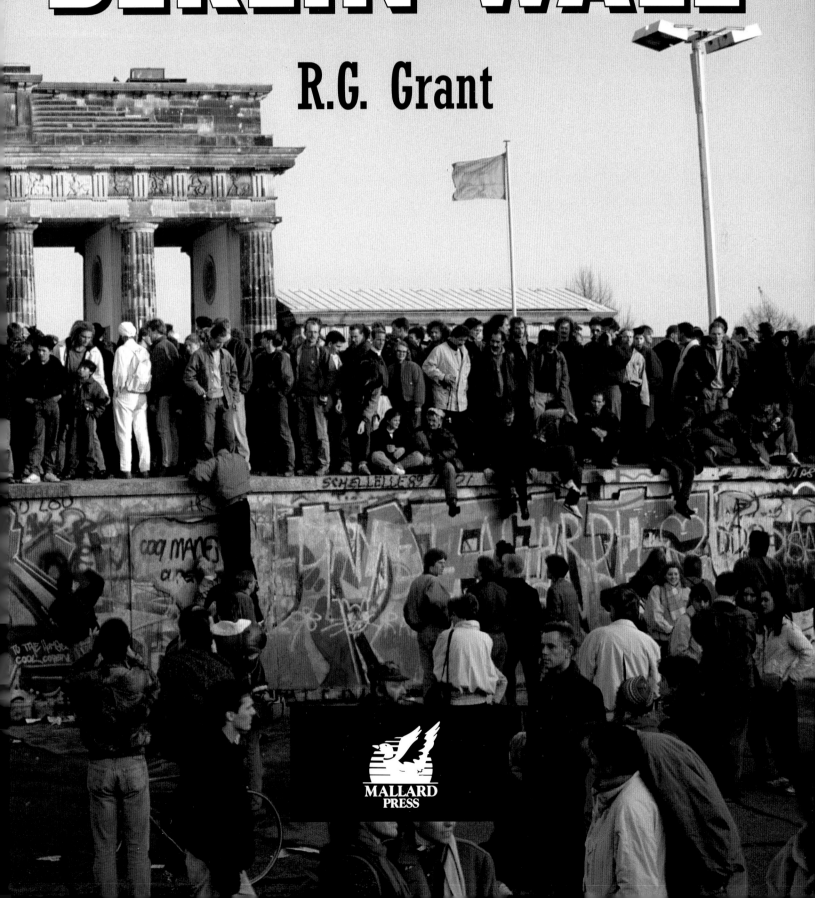

MALLARD
PRESS

First published in the United States of America in 1991
by The Mallard Press
Mallard Press and its accompanying design and logo are
trademarks of BDD Promotional Book Company, Inc.

ISBN 0-7924-5551-7

Printed in Hong Kong

PAGE 1: East and West Berliners are reunited after the
opening of the Potsdamerplatz crossing point, November 11
1989.
PAGES 2/3: The people of Berlin celebrate their triumph over
the Wall at the Brandenburg Gate.

CONTENTS

INTRODUCTION

At an auction held in late June 1990 in the Mediterranean millionaires' playground of Monaco, 81 slabs of the Berlin Wall, with due certificates of authenticity, were sold off to the world's rich and famous for over $1 million. Around the globe, everyone who was anyone had to have a piece of the Wall: Ronald Reagan now owns a section with a sprayed-on image of a pink butterfly; the Vatican, for some reason, bought a slab sprayed with the symbol of the Baader-Meinhof terrorist gang. Meanwhile tourist visitors to Berlin, lacking $20,000 to spend and with nowhere to put a ten-foot high piece of masonry in their apartments, could still find a small piece of Wall to wear as an earing or display on a shelf – though the authenticity of the fragments on sale around Potsdamerplatz and the Brandenburg Gate was as dubious as that of the splinters of the True Cross once peddled to medieval pilgrims at the shrines of Holy Jerusalem.

That the German Democratic Republic, the socialist state of East Germany, should have set up a company to auction off its Anti-Fascist Defense Wall to the rich of the West was an irony anyone could appreciate. The Wall had once stood as a symbol of Cold War confrontation; its sale was almost a caricature of the triumph of capitalism. But the auction also presented an unsettling example of trivialization and easy oblivion. Seventy-eight people had died attempting to cross this Wall, shot by border guards whose uniforms and medals were now also

up for sale, with the rest of the debris of communism, on the streets of central Berlin. An East German might legitimately ask if this was what the freedom celebrated with such glorious abandon on November 9-10 1989, the night the Wall split open, really amounted to in the end: the sale of the century. East Germany was up for grabs, a whole economy to be knocked down to the highest bidder. In November 1989 the sound of freedom had been the clink of hammers and chisels chipping away at the Wall; now it was the rap of the auctioneer's gavel.

A year after the breaching of the Wall, the wasteland where this strange fortification had once stood wound across the Berlin cityscape like scar tissue. Its abandoned watchtowers were rapidly falling into ruin, stained with graffiti, their purpose already half-forgotten. But the division of the city into East and West was still plain and stark, as indeed it had been for a decade before the Wall was built. In the East there was no concentration of smart cafés or fast-food restaurants, no porno shows or blaze of neon, no chic wealth as paraded on West Berlin's Kurfurstendamm. The inhabitants of the East were still quieter, more outwardly conformist, visibly less wealthy than their western co-citizens. Indeed, East Berlin had taken on something of the aspect of those poverty-stricken European cities on the edge of the Third World – Istanbul, perhaps, or Naples – with lines of shivering vendors on Alexanderplatz trying to sell a

RIGHT: Soviet leader Nikita Khrushchev (center) visited the Wall in January 1963, 18 months after it was built. The elderly bespectacled figure third from the left in the background of the photograph is the East German communist leader Walter Ulbricht.

LEFT: East German border guards keep watch on events in West Berlin in June 1988. By that time, the Wall had become the longest art gallery in the world, covered in paintings and graffiti.

few packets of cigarettes off upturned boxes. No one could predict how long it would take for the two halves of Berlin to grow back into one.

The Berlin of spies and Cold War confrontation had been consigned to the history books and an outdated novelistic genre, but no one knew what future awaited the re-united city, 'a place at once garish, gaunt and verdant' as writer C J Fox wonderfully described it. Was it the city's destiny to be capital of the new united Germany? Geographically it was far from the heart of Germany's population and economy, centered on the Ruhr and the Rhine far to the west. But if the country's economic destiny lay in the domination of middle and east Europe, then Berlin might yet be a key location. Some estimates foresaw a new city almost doubling in size within a decade.

LEFT: A cross and wreaths commemorate the death of 18-year-old Peter Fechter, shot by East German border guards while attempting to flee across the Wall to the West on August 17 1962. In total, 78 people are thought to have lost their lives at the Wall during the 28 years of its existence.

RIGHT: In some parts of Berlin, such as Heidelberger Strasse, the Wall followed the line of a street, dividing people from their neighbors in houses on the other side of the road.

RIGHT: In some parts of Berlin, such as Heidelberger Strasse, the Wall followed the line of a street, dividing people from their neighbors in houses on the other side of the road.

BELOW: The *S-bahn*, Berlin's elevated railway, crosses the 'death strip' behind the Wall, with the Reichstag building looming in the background. Operated by the East German state railway company, the *S-bahn* continued to run across the Wall throughout the years of a divided Berlin, although easterners could not, of course, use it to travel to the West.

The future was viewed by most Berliners with as much apprehension as expectation. For more than 40 years the West Berliners had been island dwellers, cut off from West Germany by a gray sea of communism. Now they were having to get used to being reconnected with the mainland. There were to be no more subsidies from the Bonn government after 1994 and no more exemption from military service for the young, a privilege that had made Berlin a focus for 'alternative' youth culture. The large Turkish community might find its labor no longer needed and be drafted back home. On an everyday level, there was more traffic and less space for parking, serious pressure for new building and a change to the rhythm of life.

In East Berlin a year after the fall of the Wall, the grimness of unemployment and insecurity had already struck, to temper the excitement of reunification. Very few wanted the past back again; the sight of well-stocked shops and travel agents advertising holidays in Majorca was enough to convince any East Berliner that change had been for the better. But, to take one example, easterners were still paying 20 pfennigs for their urban transport tickets, less than a tenth of the fare on the western side. The scale of the economic adjustment to be achieved was staggering.

East German teachers, civil servants, army officers, industrial managers, all found their hard-earned skills depreciated and scorned. They were lucky if they kept their jobs through 'retraining' in which they were patronized and humiliated by instructors from the West. The most unfortunate found that their homes were claimed by former proprietors who had been dispossessed by the communists or even by the Nazis. Such long-established hardships of life in the East as poor accommodation were joined by the new evils of crime and street violence – bank robberies, attacks by neo-Nazi skinheads and battles between squatters, infiltrating from West Berlin, and the police.

Meanwhile the few segments of the Wall still standing in Berlin were fought over by contending factions, those who sought to preserve at least some part of the Wall as an historical monument and a tourist attraction and the advocates of total demolition, the obliteration of all trace of the humiliation,

LEFT: In its final form the Wall was a formidable barrier, with its concrete watchtowers and powerful lighting at night. There were very few attempts at a direct crossing of the Wall by escapers after the 1960s.

division and oppression that the structure had represented. After all, the inhabitants of Berlin were not tourists, and to them the Wall had never been an attraction.

This book is, in its own way, a remembrance of the Wall. It traces the origins of the division of Berlin and of Germany after World War II, and follows the path by which that division eventually led to the Wall's construction. It shows how the dramas and tragedies of the early years of the Wall gradually modulated into a grudging acceptance and resignation, until Mikhail Gorbachev brought a fresh spring of hope and the force of popular aspirations, once released, reduced the whole structure of the communist state to a heap of rubble. As befits the story of Berlin, it contains no unambivalent heroes and no unambiguous message. But it may at least say something about how the city was in the lost age of the Cold War.

LEFT: The day after the opening of the border, November 10 1989, young Berliners climbed on to the Wall to enjoy a moment of freedom. This vantage point also gave an excellent view of the festivities.

11

1
THE CONQUERED CITY

LEFT: Soviet soldiers celebrate the conquest of
Berlin at the end of April 1945. The city was in
ruins and at the mercy of the victorious
Red Army.

In May 1945 Berlin lay in ruins, a conquered city at the mercy of its enemies. One of the great centers of European civilization and culture, the city which Adolf Hitler planned to refashion as the monumental center of his thousand-year Reich had been reduced by the Fuhrer's war to a wasteland of rubble, a charnel house of despair. Willy Brandt, a future mayor of Berlin, later described the chaos and desolation that defeat in war had brought in its wake:

Craters, caves, mountains of rubble, debris-covered fields . . . no fuel, no light, every little garden a graveyard and, above all this, like an immoveable cloud, the stink of putrefaction. In this no man's land lived human beings. Their life was a daily struggle for a handful of potatoes, a loaf of bread, a few lumps of coal, some cigarettes.

In the last two years of the war, air raids night and day by the USAF and the RAF had killed around 50,000 Berliners and rendered half the city's population homeless. Then had come the furious final battle for Berlin in the last two weeks of April 1945. Elaborating impossible fantasies of survival in the depths of his Führerbunker near Potsdamer-

platz, Hitler had ordered his people to fight to the death against the encircling Soviet forces. Schoolchildren and the elderly were forced to stand alongside the remnants of the elite of the German Army and foreign volunteers who had staked their lives on the Nazi cause. The carnage in the street fighting was among the worst in the whole of World War II. More than 100,000 civilians died as the Soviets reduced the city's defenses building by building. Families huddled together in cellars, protected from artillery fire by heaps of rubble. In the midst of the battle, housewives queued for bread wearing steel helmets; many were cut down by shrapnel or strafing aircraft. Men who attempted to end the pointless slaughter by surrender or desertion were hanged or shot out of hand by the SS. On April 30 Hitler and his mistress, now wife, Eva Braun committed suicide; an hour before midnight, Russian soldiers hung the Red Flag from the Brandenburg Gate, the symbolic heart of Berlin.

The Soviets had suffered 20,000 casualties in the battle for Berlin. In all, the war may have cost 20 million Soviet lives. The Germans had behaved with an unspeakable

BELOW: Berlin in 1945 presented a panorama of desolation. Defeat in war and the crimes of Naziism had reduced Germany to a physical, moral and psychological 'zero point', from which the whole country had to be built afresh.

inhumanity toward Soviet civilians and prisoners of war, murdering millions through massacre or deliberate neglect. In the first days of May, as the German forces laid down their arms, Soviet soldiers avenged themselves upon Berlin – not systematically, but with a random self-indulgence. As reserve and supply forces rolled into the city to join the combat troops, they were given free rein to loot and to use the local population for their sexual satisfaction. One Berlin resident, Klaus Fuhrmann, gave a typical account of the casual, almost innocent brutality of two Russian soldiers who raped his wife:

With the usual words, 'Frau komm!' spoken in a menacing voice, one of them went towards her. I was about to interfere; but the other shouted 'Stoi' and jammed his machine pistol in my chest. In my despair I shouted 'Run away, quick'; but that was, of course, impossible . . . When the first Russian had had enough they changed places. The second was chattering in Russian all the time. At last it was over. The man patted me on the shoulder: 'Nix Angst! Russki Soldat gut!'

Already deeply prejudiced against the Russians after years of Nazi propaganda denouncing the 'sub-human' Slavs, the Germans were confirmed in their fear and hatred by such experiences in the brief no man's land between war and peace.

Once discipline was re-established the Soviets instituted a systematic pillage of Berlin's resources, seizing any material or machinery that might aid the recovery of their own war-ruined economy. Railway track was torn up and carried back to the Soviet Union; so were whole factories, dismantled and transported eastward. About a half of Berlin's industrial plant that had survived the bombing was carried off in this form of instant reparations. Slowly, basic services such as water supplies and electricity were restored to the city. The Red Army set up soup kitchens to feed the starving population. At the same time the military authorities hunted for former Nazis,

ABOVE: A Soviet military policewoman directs traffic in front of the battle-scarred Brandenburg Gate in May 1945. Many buildings in Berlin still bear the marks of bullets and shrapnel today.

members of the Hitler Youth, Wehrmacht officers or NCOs, relying on denunciations from the victims of Nazi persecution or arresting men at random for investigation. Several hundred thousand were imprisoned in camps; an estimated 96,000 were executed or died of neglect. Many of those executed were guilty of appalling crimes; more were probably not.

The period of Soviet occupation of all Berlin lasted only two months. Although the Soviets alone had fought to take the city, they were not to be allowed exclusive possession of it. The supreme commander of the Western Allied forces, General Dwight D. Eisenhower, had been quite happy to let the Red Army suffer the grim toll of casualties in the final assault on the heart of Hitler's Reich, confident that the division of Berlin and the rest of Germany between the Allies would be determined by diplomatic

agreements, not by the position of the armies at the cessation of hostilities.

The fate of Berlin had been decided in outline at a series of wartime meetings between the Allied powers from 1943 onward. Stalin, Roosevelt and Churchill had agreed that Germany must never again be allowed to threaten the peace of the world. Various ideas were floated as to how this might be achieved, from splitting the country into smaller fragments to transforming it into an impoverished nation of peasant farmers, but it was settled that, in the immediate aftermath of the war, the country should be occupied by the Allies and subjected to their joint military rule. It would not be permitted military forces and its industries would be partially dismantled. The Soviet armed forces were to occupy Germany east of the Elbe, Britain the northwest of the country including the Ruhr, and the United States the southwest; as a later afterthought, a zone was also found for the French. Berlin lay deep within the zone designated for Soviet occupation, but the Allies agreed to share the capital on the same basis as the rest of Germany it would be divided between the Allies into separate occupied sectors.

No one envisaged the division into zones of military occupation as more than a temporary measure for the transitional period between war and peace. Even during that period, Germany and Berlin were to be administered jointly by the occupying powers, although each ally would have special responsibilities in its own zone. The military authorities would disarm the Germans and carry out a de-Nazification program, arrange the payment of reparations and eventually supervise the implementation of a peace treaty which would restore Germany to some form of independence.

The actual dividing lines for the occupation of Berlin were decided in the London Protocol of September 12 1944, slightly modified two months later. It was agreed to split the city along traditional district (*'Bezirke'*) boundaries. Eight easterly districts were allotted to Soviet occupation forces, including the Mitte, the central area of Berlin around Unter den Linden. The rest of the city was divided between the French in the north, the British in the center and the Americans in the south. The Soviet sector covered almost exactly one half the area of Berlin but contained only one third of the city's population. It was assumed that the Soviets and the other Allies would administer the city harmoniously together; no thought was given to the implications of the division should the Allies fall out.

LEFT: Churchill, Truman and Stalin, the leaders of the victorious wartime alliance, meet at Potsdam, in the outskirts of Berlin, in July 1945. Behind the smiles there was deep distrust, and the alliance between East and West was not long to survive the onset of peace.

After the German surrender at the end of the first week of May 1945, the agreements were observed virtually to the letter. By the time Stalin, Truman and Churchill gathered in the Cecilienhof Palace at Potsdam, on the outskirts of Berlin, in the middle of July 1945, Western troops had already joined the Soviets in Berlin. The Potsdam meeting confirmed earlier agreements on the occupation of Germany and finalized in detail the exact manner in which the military government would work. The administration of the whole country was to be overseen by an Allied Control Council composed of the four

LEFT: A Red Army military band marches down Unter den Linden, in the center of Berlin, as part of a parade celebrating victory in Europe. Faithful to his agreements with the West, Stalin allowed British, French and American troops to join the Red Army in the occupation of the city.

RIGHT: American troops march into Berlin in June 1945 to occupy the southwest sector of the city. No one imagined that the US Army was going to stay for almost half a century.

victorious powers; there would also be a combined four-power military council, the Kommandatura, to administer the city of Berlin. There were already points of difference between the victorious powers on the German issue: Britain and the United States were unhappy at Stalin's unilateral decision to fix a new eastern border for Germany, transferring East Prussia and Silesia to Poland, and taking a small slice for the Soviet Union (Germany lost roughly one quarter of its 1937 land area). The Soviets also wanted more reparations from Germany than the Western powers believed

RIGHT: The Allied armies taking over the ruined city discovered a traumatized population, largely women, children and the elderly, almost all of whom had suffered bereavement and witnessed violent death.

LEFT: Berlin was desperately short of supplies of every kind in the aftermath of the war. Disease, malnutrition and lack of heating and shelter took their toll, especially of the elderly and young children.

BELOW: Women were organized into labor gangs to clear away the bricks and masonry from demolished buildings. They were known in German as *Trümmerfrauen* (women of the ruins).

were practicable. But these were details that did little to mar the general accord.

The arrival of British, French and American soldiers in Berlin was greeted with relief by the local population. The Western powers were not necessarily any more inclined to treat the Germans well than were the Soviets. At the end of the war, for instance, many thousands of German POWs were allowed to die of starvation and disease in American and French camps. But a large majority of the German population was fixed in its preference for the West, and this was to prove a major factor in the post-war history of Germany and of Berlin. Millions of Germans had fled westward as the Soviet forces advanced. The Germans driven out of East Prussia and Silesia mostly made the long journey to the zones under American or British control, as did two million Germans from the Sudetenland in Czechoslovakia. By 1946 there were about eight million refugees in western Germany. People also flowed west from the Soviet-occupied eastern zone of Germany, a movement which was destined to continue uninterrupted from the end of the war until the building of the Wall.

In the immediate postwar years, conditions of life were grim and harsh throughout Germany, but nowhere was life harder than in Berlin. With productive economic activity at a halt, the local population had little but the charity of the occupying forces on which

RIGHT: The ruins stank of decaying bodies buried in the rubble, but clearing the ground was the first necessary step toward restoring a semblance of normal life. The Allied soldiers who oversaw the work at first tended to take a punitive attitude toward the hated Germans, but most were softened by everyday contacts and the visible evidence of suffering and hardship.

to stay alive. Conditions were worst in the Soviet sector. Itself in ruins and desperately impoverished, the Soviet Union saw no reason to waste supplies on a defeated enemy that had laid waste Soviet cities and countryside. But even in the Western sectors, rations were set at levels that guaranteed malnutrition. Clearing the acres of rubble was a massive task. Gangs of undernourished women – almost all the men were either dead or prisoners of war – labored wearily to clear the bricks and stones by hand. Transported to the outskirts of the city, the bricks were piled into hills like slag heaps. (They came in handy when the decision was made to build the Wall in 1961: the rapidly constructed first version was mostly built out of crushed brick that had once been pre-war Berlin.)

Much of the population was sheltering in cellars or the ruined shells of buildings. They were traumatized by the experience of the bombing and occupation. In the disloca-

tion of war, almost everyone had lost touch with a spouse, children or friends. Throughout the city, people left notices scrawled on cardboard in a desperate attempt to find those who had disappeared. There were bodies everywhere, rotting amid the ruins. Diseases such as typhoid, dysentery and tuberculosis ravaged a weakened population. During the viciously cold winter of 1946-47, wolves were seen in the Berlin streets and over 50,000 people were treated for frostbite. Children risked their lives to steal a few lumps of coal from stocks defended by Western or Soviet soldiers.

Crime and corruption were universal. On the flourishing black market whose traders packed Alexanderplatz, Potsdamerplatz and the Brandenburg Gate, survival was for sale – for those who could find anything to trade or sell. American or British soldiers could have almost anything they desired. Powerless and on the point of starvation, Berliners would exchange valuables or sex for the simplest of life's luxuries – cigarettes, alcohol – that the soldiers had to offer. Morally there was little to choose between this exploitation of poverty and the Soviet soldier's habit of taking what he wanted by force, but it did not make the Western armies as unpopular. Cynical though it may be, and Berlin is a cynical city, it was better to be bought with chocolate and cigarettes than robbed or raped at the point of a gun.

By 1947 it was clear that the occupying powers could not go on administering Germany as a conquered country indefinitely. Keeping the Germans down would prove too expensive, too destructive and too inhumane. The British, in particular, soon recognized the hopelessness of a policy designed to restrict German economic recovery, as they found themselves pumping essential supplies into the Ruhr and into their sector of Berlin at a moment when, at home, rationing was worse than at any time during the war. An impoverished Britain could not afford to pay to keep the Germans alive, yet nor could they leave the Germans to starve. In some way, the defeated enemy had to be restored to self-government and enabled once more to feed itself.

It was difficult to bring about any change, however, unless the four wartime allies could agree on a future shape for Germany. This they could not. In the two years after the German surrender, interminable meetings of the four-power Council of Foreign Ministers – Ernest Bevin for Britain, General George C. Marshall representing the United States, Vyacheslav Molotov of the Soviet Union and Georges Bidault for France –

ABOVE: Much of the Berlin population was homeless, living on the streets.

LEFT: Soviet soldiers distribute bread rations to Berlin civilians. Without the food supplied by the occupying armies, millions of Germans would have starved.

OPPOSITE: Standing in food lines took up much of the day for the citizens of Berlin. Two years after the end of the war, the official rations were still set at a level barely adequate to support life.

BELOW: Berliners pick over garbage thrown out by the US Army, looking for anything that is edible or might serve as fuel.

failed to make any significant progress toward a final settlement. Both the Soviet Union and the Western powers were committed to the creation of a united, demilitarized Germany under international supervision, the Soviets favoring a more centralized form of government, the West preferring a loose federal structure. But each side feared that the other might achieve control of this new state, a prospect they found intolerable as East-West tension mounted toward Cold War. In the absence of agreement, there was a strong temptation for each side to impose its own political and economic solution on the area of Germany under its military control.

Which side was initially responsible for splitting Germany in two has been the subject of historical dispute ever since. The Soviets were certainly quick to move toward a Stalinist system in their own occupation zone. A planeload of German communists, politicians who had fled to the Soviet Union from Hitler's Reich in the 1930s and had spent the war in Moscow, were flown into Berlin on April 30 1945, while the battle for

the capital was still raging. They included Walter Ulbricht, an uninspiring timeserver who could be relied upon to toe the line laid down by Stalin (he had applauded the Nazi-Soviet Pact of 1939) and who was to emerge as the dominant figure in communist East Germany. Before Hitler banned the party in 1933, there had been mass popular support for the communists in working-class areas of Germany, especially in Berlin. Many people were ready to resume their communist allegiance after the war, but not in sufficient numbers to allow a communist victory in democratic elections. The Soviets had to coerce German society into the shape they required. All major businesses and estates over 250 acres were confiscated, and a communist-led police force was set up with its headquarters in Berlin. A rigorous campaign of de-Nazification, which also gathered in its net many who had not been Nazis but were potential opponents of a communist regime, was followed by a drive to force other political parties with wider popular support to join a communist-dominated alliance.

The most popular party, as German political life tentatively revived in the aftermath of the war, was the German Social Democratic Party (Sozialdemokratische Partei Deutschlands, SPD), which adhered to Marxist principles and advocated a program of sweeping nationalization, but which used impeccably democratic methods. In the Soviet sector the SPD was put under a great deal of pressure to ally with the communists and, in March 1946, its local leader, Otto Grotewohl, agreed to merge with the Communist Party to form the Socialist Unity Party (Sozialistische Einheitspartei Deutschlands, SED). But other SPD leaders, including Kurt Schumacher at a national level and Ernst Reuter in Berlin, were hostile to the communists. Reuter was himself a former communist who remembered with great bitterness the behavior of the Party in the early 1930s, when it had denounced the democratic socialists as 'social Fascists' instead of uniting in resistance to Hitler. Reuter and other SPD leaders in the Western-occupied sectors of Berlin organized a referendum on Grotewohl's policy: over 80 percent of social democrats opposed the merger with the communists, although a majority favored close cooperation between the two main strands of the German left. Thus in the Western sectors the SPD remained independent.

In October 1946 elections were held in all four sectors for a Berlin City Assembly, the only citywide democratic elections between 1933 and 1990. The SED, identified with the deeply unpopular Soviet occupation forces, won only 26 of the 130 seats; Ernst Reuter's SPD were the clear victors. The City Assembly met in the Soviet sector and tactfully elected an executive body, the Magistrat, which included representatives of the SED and the two other main parties as well as the victorious SPD. Nonetheless, when Ernst Reuter was elected to head the city government as Burgomeister, the Soviet authorities refused to validate the decision. His deputies Luise Schroeder and Ferdinand Friedensburg temporarily took his place.

While the Soviets consolidated the dominant position of communism in the East, the Western Allies shifted toward the economic and political integration of the rest of Germany. In January 1947 the British and American zones were merged into a single economic unit; the French zone did not join until later, the French being considerably more reluctant than Britain or the United States to witness a revival of German power. At the same time de-Nazification, which had weighed heavily on industrialists and civil servants compromised by dealings with Hitler's regime, was halted or reversed. The immediate motive behind these moves was to help restore German industry and agriculture, which in turn would relieve the occupying powers of the burden of support-

RIGHT: In the absence of any normal economic activity, the black market flourished in postwar Berlin. Here, traders caught selling black market goods are arrested and taken away in the back of a police truck.

ing the local population and contribute to a general revival of the European economy, still slumped in postwar depression. But the idea of forming western Germany into a bulwark, or even an ally, against Soviet communism was already stirring beneath the surface. There had been contacts between some German military and intelligence officers and their Western opposite numbers even before the war ended, seeking to align Germany with the West against the Soviet Union. In the immediate postwar period such a notion was still taboo at a higher political level, at least in public. But the Western-occupied zones held the lion's share of Germany, about 70 percent of its population and most of its heavy industry. There was a strong logic to abandoning the impoverished, largely agricultural east of Germany to the Soviets, in return for excluding communism from the rest.

By the start of 1948, relations between the Soviet Union and the Western Allies had reached breaking point. The United States was overtly organizing a ring of friendly powers around the Soviet sphere of influence to 'contain communism'. Soviet behavior in Eastern Europe, culminating in the communist takeover in Czechoslovakia in the spring of 1948, was alien to Western principles of freedom and democracy. Despairing of reaching an agreement with the Soviets, in February 1948 the United States, Britain and France met in London to con-

sider plans for the creation of a German government in their occupation zones. In response the following month Marshal Vasili Sokolovsky, the Soviet Military Governor in Germany, walked out of the Allied Control Council, protesting that the behavior of the Western powers proved 'they no longer considered the Control Commission to be the four-power authority in Germany'.

ABOVE: Ernst Reuter, the socialist head of the Berlin city government, led the popular resistance to Soviet attempts to take over the city. His brave and resolute stance encouraged the Western Allies to maintain their military presence in West Berlin.

LEFT: In 1945 the four occupying powers marked the boundaries of their respective sectors of Berlin with signboards, but there were few restrictions on movement between the sectors. The division of the city was assumed to be a temporary arrangement.

As the split between Soviet- and Western-occupied Germany widened, Berlin was stranded in an incongruous and precarious situation. The city was 120 miles from the nearest point in the American zone of western Germany, it was actually closer to the new border of Poland. British, American and French forces had the right of access to their sectors of the city through the Soviet zone by road, rail and air. But if the pretence at a unified Allied occupation of Germany was abandoned, access could easily be blocked by Soviet forces. The 6500 Western troops in Berlin and the 2.5 million German inhabitants of the Western sectors of the city were effectively hostages in Soviet hands.

On April 1 1948 a train carrying US troops and German civilians to Berlin was halted as it entered the Soviet zone. Soviet officers demanded to examine the Americans' documents, in contravention of existing agreements which allowed all the occupying forces to travel freely without showing their papers. To avoid a confrontation, the

US Military Governor General Lucius D Clay ordered his men to comply, but a gauntlet had been thrown down. From that point onward, a Soviet campaign of harassment repeatedly slowed or interrupted passage on communication routes into Berlin. Western military leaders were not at all sure that this exposed outpost in Soviet-controled Eastern Europe was worth holding on to. On April 10 General Omar Bradley, the US Army Chief of Staff, expressed doubts as to 'whether our people are prepared to start a war to maintain our position in Berlin', and asked if it might not be preferable to 'announce withdrawal and minimize loss of prestige rather than being forced out by threat?' But General Clay was adamant: 'If we mean we are to hold Europe against communism, ' he told the Pentagon, 'we must not budge . . .' Already Berlin had become what it was to remain for almost half a century: a symbolic counter in the Cold War game.

Matters came to a head in a battle over currencies. On June 20 the Western powers

BELOW: In August 1945, Western and Soviet military leaders and diplomats take the air after the first meeting of the Allied Control Council, the body that was intended to provide a united administration for occupied Germany. On the far left is Marshal Sokolovsky, the Soviet representative on the Council. Between Field Marshal Montgomery and General Eisenhower is the Soviet war hero Marshal Georgi Zhukov.

LEFT: On September 6 1948, in the Soviet sector of Berlin, a communist-inspired crowd prevented the City Assembly from meeting in the Neues Stadthaus. The Assembly's non-communist majority moved their session to the Schöneberg Rathaus in West Berlin.

BELOW: Ernst Reuter addressed a mass demonstration in front of the Reichstag building on September 9 1948, affirming the determination of the people of Berlin to resist Soviet domination.

introduced a new Deutschmark in the zones under their control. This currency reform immediately killed off the black market and was destined eventually to lay the foundations for the German 'economic miracle'. From the Soviet point of view, the introduction of the Deutschmark was a hostile act, the decisive step toward the creation of an independent capitalist West Germany. They countered by launching their own new East Zone currency. On June 22 Marshal Sokolovsky announced that the Soviet-backed Mark would be the sole valid currency in Berlin, and that the city 'had been integrated economically into the Soviet zone'. The Western powers rejected the Soviet claims to the city and insisted that their Deutschmark would circulate in the Western sectors.

For Berliners it was a decisive moment. On June 23 the city government, led by Reuter's deputy Luise Schroeder, rejected the Soviet proposal and called for the eastern currency to be restricted to the Soviet sector. This was a courageous decision. The City Assembly and its leaders, meeting inside the Soviet sector, were exposed to constant threats of violence and offered no protection by the police. If the Western powers chose to abandon Berlin, Reuter, Schroeder and their colleagues knew they would face a grim fate. Yet they also knew they had the support of the overwhelming majority of the Berlin population in resisting absorption into the Soviet zone. Just before midnight

on June 23, the Soviet-controled news agency ADN issued a short statement:

The Transport Division of the Soviet Military Administration is forced to halt all passenger and freight traffic to and from Berlin as from 0600 hours tomorrow because of technical problems.

With this terse lie, the Berlin blockade began. The following morning all road and rail links between West Berlin and the outside world were cut.

Stalin did not want war. He intended to offer the Western powers a choice: they could halt progress toward the economic and political independence of West Germany and keep their share in Berlin, or they could sacrifice Berlin and continue the drive to West German independence. There were many political and military leaders in Washington who felt the second option made sense. The Western outpost in Berlin was exposed, indefensible and of no practical use; now that the Iron Curtain had been drawn across central Europe, Berlin must fall into the Soviet sphere. The commanders on the ground in Berlin, however, saw things differently. They were in daily contact with the city's inhabitants and their

political spokesmen. They knew that the people of Berlin were prepared to resist the imposition of Soviet-backed communist rule at almost any cost. On June 24 some 80,000 people gathered in the center of the city to demonstrate their opposition to a Soviet takeover. Ernst Reuter expressed the common feeling in a ringing declaration of hostility to Stalinism:

With all the means at our disposal we shall fight those who want to turn us into slaves and helots of a party. We have lived under such slavery in the days of Adolf Hitler. We want no return to such times . . .

In private consultations, Reuter made it plain to western officials in Berlin that the local population would fight any Soviet attempt to absorb the rest of the city, whether the West supported them or not. The Berliners' determined will to resist stiffened the resolve of the British and American authorities.

But exactly how the Soviet blockade could be answered was not immediately evident. Food stocks in the Western sectors were only adequate to supply the population for 36 days, even at the very low level

BELOW: In June 1948, new currencies were introduced in both the Soviet and Western zones of Germany, and lines developed outside banks as people queued for their new Marks. This was the scene in East Berlin – note the street name in Cyrillic lettering, for the benefit of Soviet soldiers.

of rations then in force. Most of Berlin's electricity came from the Soviet sector and was cut off once the blockade started. There was enough coal in the Western sectors to keep their power stations operating for 45 days. After that, the city faced cold, darkness and starvation.

Initially the hawkish General Clay adopted an overtly aggressive posture; he intended to call the Soviets' bluff. 'The Russians . . .', he told journalists, 'can't drive us out of Berlin by anything short of war'. Clay had made plans to assemble a supply convoy of 200 trucks and launch it along the Helmstedt-Berlin autobahn with a powerful military escort. If the Soviets tried to enforce the blockade and stop the convoy, the escort would have orders to blast its way through. The Soviets would be confronted with a choice between lifting the blockade and open warfare.

Perhaps fortunately for the future of mankind, the British put forward an alternative plan that ran less risk of starting World War III. The Soviets had made no move to block the air corridors across the Soviet zone into Berlin. An RAF officer, Air Commodore Waite, persuaded the British Military Governor, General Sir Brian Robertson, that it might be possible to supply not only the military garrison but the entire population by air. General Clay was far from convinced that an airlift would work, but on June 25 he

agreed to give it a chance. 'I may be the craziest man in the world,' he told Reuter, 'but I'm going to try the experiment of feeding this city by air'.

The immediate prospects did not look good. The population of 2.5 million would need approximately 4500 tonnes of supplies a day. Each of the USAF's C-47 Dakotas, their standard transport aircraft, could carry a load of less than three tonnes, and there were only 102 Dakotas stationed in Europe. On June 26, the first day of the airlift, the US 61st Transport Group, flying out of Wiesbaden in West Germany, transported just 80 tonnes of supplies into Tempelhof airbase in the American sector of Berlin. As other aircraft joined in – C-54 Skymasters drafted into Europe from as far off as Hawaii and Alaska, RAF Sunderland flying boats that could land on the Havel lakes in the Berlin suburbs, converted Lancasters to transport liquid fuel – the tonnage carried rose steeply. With new runways built at Tempelhof and at Gatow in the British sector, 2000 tonnes a day of supplies were flowing into Berlin by the end of July. In mid-August daily deliveries for the first time outstripped the 4500 tonnes considered necessary for the city's survival. As the volume of traffic increased, the problems of organizing flight control, servicing aircraft and moving goods on such a huge scale became formidable, but technical barriers were all that the pilots

ABOVE: During the Berlin airlift, seaplanes landed on the Havel lakes on the outskirts of Berlin, ferrying in essential supplies to help sustain the population in the Western sectors of the city.

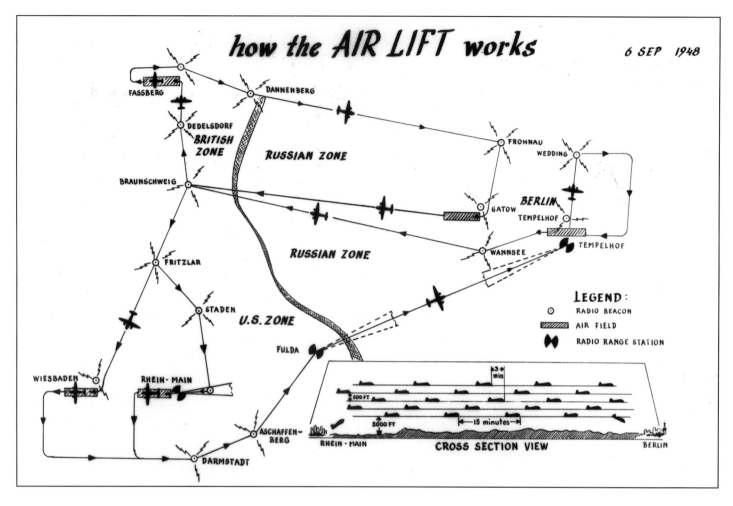

how the AIR LIFT works   6 SEP 1948

FASSBERG
DANNENBERG
DEDELSDORF
BRITISH ZONE
RUSSIAN ZONE
FROHNAU
WEDDING
BRAUNSCHWEIG
BERLIN
GATOW
TEMPELHOF
TEMPELHOF
RUSSIAN ZONE
WANNSEE
FRITZLAR
LEGEND:
○ RADIO BEACON
▨ AIR FIELD
☯ RADIO RANGE STATION
STADEN
U.S. ZONE
FULDA
WIESBADEN
RHEIN-MAIN
CROSS SECTION VIEW
ASCHAFFEN-BERG
RHEIN-MAIN
±3 min
500 FT
5000 FT
15 minutes
BERLIN
DARMSTADT

ABOVE: The Berlin airlift was a masterpiece of logistical organization, as this contemporary information document shows. With only two airports to fly into, at Tempelhof and Gatow, and restricted to narrow air corridors across the Soviet zone, the pilots and air traffic controllers had to maintain perfect discipline to avoid hold-ups or, at worst, mid-air collisions. The pilots navigated chiefly by homing in on fixed-point radio beacons.

and flight crews had to overcome. Despite occasional threats and 'buzzing' by Soviet fighters, the Soviet Air Force made no attempt to block the air corridors.

The drone and throb of transport aircraft swooping in over the Berlin rooftops, two a minute at the height of the airlift, became as much a part of the Berlin landscape as the gaunt ruins of buildings in the city center and the queues for rationed foodstuffs. Life had recovered little in the three years since the end of the war; the blockade brought fresh hardships and deprivation. Rations averaged about 1800 calories a day, with almost no fresh meat or vegetables. Berliners headed out into the countryside in search of food but on returning to the city they were often shaken down by Soviet guards and relieved of a few precious potatoes they had hidden in their pockets.

There was a chronic shortage of fuel. At the beginning of the siege, the Western military authorities announced that two-thirds of the Grünewald forest on the outskirts of the city was to be cut down and distributed as firewood, along with half of West Berlin's other trees in streets and parks. Most of such industry as had survived bombing and Soviet dismantling now closed down. Electricity for domestic use was restricted to two hours in the morning

and another two-hour period in the evening. Street lighting was cut by 75 percent and electric-powered public transport – trams and the underground railway – stopped at 6 pm. Shop windows were dark and illuminated signs went out. As the freezing autumn fogs closed in, Berlin was a bleak, fearful city. Morale in the Western sectors remained surprisingly high, the experience of righteous resistance to Soviet pressure revived a population demoralized by defeat. On July 20, the Soviet authorities offered full rations to any citizen from West Berlin who was prepared to register in the Soviet sector. Only four percent of the population took advantage of this offer, even when the blockade was at its tightest.

Although the fate of the city was in the hands of outside powers, a political battle for control of Berlin developed around the City Assembly. On July 26 the SPD-dominated administration sacked the Berlin police chief, Colonel Paul Markgraf, who had been taking orders from the Soviets and the communists rather than from the elected city authorities. The Soviets refused to accept Markgraf's dismissal and reinstated him; his city-appointed replacement took office in West Berlin. Police officers not accepting Markgraf's orders became a target for Soviet retribution. On two occasions

Soviet troops raiding black marketeers on Potsdamerplatz, where the Soviet, British and American sectors met, crossed on to the Western side in hot pursuit and then abducted Western-sector policemen who fell into their hands. When such incidents occurred, the Western occupation forces were tempted to intervene against the Soviet soldiers. There was a real risk that fighting would break out between East and West on the streets of Berlin. Meanwhile Markgraf's police allowed communist-organized crowds to intimidate and molest representatives to the City Assembly, which was still holding its sessions in the Neues Stadthaus inside the Soviet sector. On September 6 rioters invaded the building and broke up the Assembly. In protest three days later a quarter of a million people crammed into the area between the ruined Reichstag and the Brandenburg Gate to listen to speeches denouncing the communists. In the excited, angry atmosphere a young demonstrator tore the Red Flag from the Brandenburg Gate and Soviet soldiers guarding the Red Army war memorial, sited in the British sector, were stoned by the crowd. Soviet troops responded by opening fire on demonstrators on their side of the Brandenburg Gate, killing one person and injuring 30.

After September 6, the majority of the City Assembly and its administration, minus the SED representatives, transferred their sessions to the Schöneberg Rathaus in the British sector. There they called fresh elections, in defiance of Soviet wishes. The communists did everything in their power to stop the elections being held, including spreading rumors that there would be a complete Soviet takeover if the poll went ahead. But on December 5 84 percent of Berlin electors cast their vote for the SPD and the two other non-communist parties, the Christian Democrats and the Liberal Democrats. A new administration, headed by Reuter, established its authority in West Berlin; on November 30, Friedrich Ebert, son of the founder of the Weimar Republic, became mayor of the Soviet sector on behalf of the SED. By the end of 1948 almost all essential services were being run by separate organizations in the East and the West. Berlin had split in two.

The commitment of the Western Allies to retaining West Berlin was strengthened with every day of the airlift. It had become the prime dramatization of the incipient Cold War, a rallying focus for popular anxieties and political will. Every available resource was thrown into the airlift. By mid-September average deliveries were over

ABOVE: German school-children watch as a USAF transport aircraft lands at Tempelhof in the American sector of Berlin. The airlift cemented a close relationship between the West German people, including West Berliners, and their former enemy, the United States.

RIGHT: After the lifting of the Soviet blockade in May 1949, *Wurst* (sausage) and fresh meat reappeared in the shop windows of West Berlin, attracting the avid attention of citizens used to a near starvation diet.

6000 tonnes a day, enough to build up stocks for the winter when bad weather would inevitably hamper flying. By the time USAF General Curtis LeMay and Britain's Air Marshal Sir Arthur Saunders merged their separate operations to form a Combined Airlift Task Force in mid-October, they were moderately confident of sustaining success. With the technology available at the time, it was far more difficult than it is today to operate in low cloud and poor visibility. The fogs of November reduced deliveries to 3000 tonnes a day and accident casualties mounted. By the end of the blockade, 54 Allied airmen had lost their lives in the airlift. But with courage and ingenuity, and the immense technical and financial resources of the United States, the problems of winter weather were overcome.

Many people on the Allied side were conscious of the ironies of a situation in which two air forces that had spent several years bombing Berlin flat were now devoting themselves to keeping its population alive. Not all the aircrews were enthusiastic about their changed role. *Newsweek* quoted one American airman as telling a journalist in October:

What I try to do now is to fly one flight a day instead of two. That way I beat those bastards in Berlin out of 10,000 pounds of coal a day.

But on the whole the spectacle of the airlift helped change popular perceptions of Ger-

many in the West, encouraging an identification with the old enemy, soon to become a new ally, and transfering hostility to an old ally, the Soviet Union, now defined as the enemy. Most Berliners survived the hard winter of 1948-49, and by February deliveries of supplies were running at about 8000 tonnes a day; the Soviet strategy had failed. On March 21 the Soviet delegate at the United Nations dropped the first hint that the blockade might be lifted. After negotiations between the four occupying powers, the Soviets agreed on 8 May to restore land access to Berlin. At 5.32 am on May 12 the first train from the West arrived in West Berlin to a tumultuous welcome. As a precaution against a sudden reimposition of the blockade, the airlift continued until the end of September. By then it was clear that Stalin had accepted defeat; Berlin would remain a divided city.

The Western Allies had struggled hard to maintain themselves in Berlin, but their victory did not render the situation any less anomalous; if anything, political developments made it more so. On May 23 1949 a 'Basic Law', drawn up by a Parliamentary Council in Bonn, established a Federal Republic in the British, French and American occupation zones. On October 7 the Soviet zone declared itself the German Democratic Republic (GDR), with Berlin as its capital. Each of the new regimes claimed to represent the whole of Germany and rejected its rival as the puppet of a foreign power; neither had full sovereignty, the occupying powers maintaining their military presence and retaining control over certain areas of state policy.

The success of the airlift left West Berlin an island in the communist GDR, a shattered fragment of the capitalist West buried in the flesh of Eastern Europe. Its exposed position as a hostage in every Cold War crisis undermined its potential for rebirth. The Federal government chose Bonn as its capital city, depriving Berlin of the rich pickings of employment at the center of state bureaucracy. The city's industry was in ruins and unlikely to attract a flood of fresh investment; political insecurity and its isolation from sources of raw materials and markets made it a dubious proposition. Paradoxically, its only strength lay in its weakness: the Federal government, not prepared to see West Berlin collapse, had to provide the funds to restore it to life. The West German taxpayer footed the bill.

The division of Germany was not the product of a deliberate plan, but it suited the Western powers well enough. By reducing the country's size, it allayed fears of a resurgence of German power, while aligning by far the greater part of Germany on the Western side of the Cold War divide. The West Germans found the fact of division hard to accept. The Basic Law of the Federal Republic was explicitly intended 'for a transitional period'; that is, until Germany should be reunified and a constitution drafted for the whole state. Nor did the Basic Law accept the loss of the eastern areas of Germany to Poland. But in practice West German leaders knew that their own power and plans for national reconstruction depended on integration into the Western world. As late as 1952, Stalin was still offering to negotiate a deal for a united, neutral, demilitarized Germany, exactly similar to the agreement successfully negotiated for Austria. But the Western powers would have nothing to do with it, and the Federal government itself regretfully declined. A divided Germany became an apparently immovable fact of European life.

The Federal Republic was established as a liberal democracy on the Western model, with competing political parties and

BELOW: The view from the roof of the Reichstag as a million demonstrators call for freedom in Berlin. The firm wish of most Berliners not to become part of a communist state was the key factor in maintaining West Berlin as an outpost of liberal democracy behind the Iron Curtain.

ABOVE: American airmen and ground crews celebrate the successful end of the airlift. Fifty-four Allied airmen died in the course of the operation, mainly as a result of accidents in bad weather conditions.

nomic miracle, created a brash individualist society, in stark contrast to the style of East Germany.

Although in theory a multi-party democracy, the GDR adopted the classic features of a Stalinist state. The official leaders were Wilhelm Pieck, head of the Council of State, and Otto Grotewohl, chairman of the Council of Ministers, but Walter Ulbricht exercised real power as secretary-general of the SED. A secret police force, the notorious Staatssicherheitsdienst (Stasi), was established with the help of the Soviet NKVD. The depressing routine of Stalinist purges began as early as 1948, when those regarded as 'Titoists' were expelled en masse from the ruling party. With each new heresy denounced from Moscow, a new batch of communists came under ban. But the harshest effects of party rule fell upon the former bourgeoisie – teachers or lawyers, landowners or businessmen, pre-1945 civil servants, officers or NCOs from the Wehrmacht. Barred from all but the most menial jobs, facing suspicion, harassment or imprisonment, thousands of highly qualified professionals fled to the West.

Whereas the United States pumped money into the West German economy through the Marshall Plan, the Soviet Union bled the East German economy. Until 1954 about one quarter of the GDR's output was confiscated by the Soviets to shore up their own war-devastated economy. In the classic Stalinist mode, the rebuilding of East Germany under the Five-Year Plan of 1950 concentrated on developing heavy industry rather than on improving living standards. Workers were encouraged to greater efforts not by the lure of higher wages but by moral exhortation and appeals to discipline. East Germany had its own equivalent of the Soviet 'Stakhanovite' work heroes, the 'Hennecke activists', named after Adolf Hennecke who had been singled out as a model of dedication in the drive to build socialism.

It is only too easy to be cynical about the GDR, but it did have an appeal to some Germans who had fled or suffered under the Nazis. Among prominent intellectuals, the novelists Anna Seghers and Stefan Heym, the philosopher Ernst Bloch and the poet and playwright Bertolt Brecht all chose East Germany as their home in the early 1950s. So did many German Jews returning from exile. They were troubled by the degree of continuity between the Federal Republic and the Nazi state; the resurgence of industrial companies (often thinly disguised) that had profited from the Holocaust, for

guarantees of freedom of expression and movement, although the political extremes of left and right did not enjoy the tolerance accorded in more stable democracies. To the surprise of most observers, more of the electorate in 1949 voted for the Christian Democrats, led by Konrad Adenauer, than for Schumacher's SPD; Adenauer became the first Chancellor of the new Republic, in a coalition with the Free Democrats. This was a decisive moment in the development of the new Germany. Schumacher had opposed 'American imperialism' and advocated extensive nationalization of industry. Under Adenauer, a conservative of rigidly authoritarian temper, West Germany gravitated into the American-led Western alliance and the economy was rebuilt through a resurgence of capitalist enterprise. The *Wirtschaftswunder*, the eco-

example, and the persistence of ex-Nazi functionaries in the higher ranks of the civil service. West Germans, of course, were more inclined to see a resemblance between Hitler's Germany and Ulbricht's: the single-party state, the secret police, the lack of democracy and fundamental freedoms.

The Berlin airlift had provided West Germany and West Berlin with a founding myth, a dramatized version that made a

satisfactory sense of their situation. It allowed their rulers and citizens to define themselves as standing resolutely for freedom against oppression and for national independence against foreign domination. The complex and muddled situation of West Berlin was simplified to a gross political antithesis: an island of freedom in a sea of tyranny. The airlift also cast the Western armed forces, in theory occupying armies on the same footing as the Soviets, as valiant friends of German freedom and independence. Their presence in West Germany was justified to the popular imagination.

The critical event that founded East Germany's sense of identity and dramatized its relations with the occupying forces came later and was of a quite different kind. It was the suppression of the workers' uprising of June 1953. Students of Soviet history were not over-surprised to see a communist regime confirmed in power by the defeat of a workers' rebellion rather than its triumph. The uprising had its roots in simmering discontent with the imposition of communist party rule, the loss of trade union rights, the continuing occupation by the Soviet Army, and the failure of living standards to rise quickly enough from the abject poverty of the immediate postwar years. The death of Stalin on March 5 1953 had raised some hopes of a change for the better, but none occurred. On June 16 the government announced that work norms, the amount of labor demanded from each worker, were

LEFT: Konrad Adenauer, leader of the Christian Democrat party, addresses the people of West Berlin in May 1949. Adenauer was soon to be elected the first Chancellor of the new Federal Republic, a post he held until 1963.

LEFT: A significant number of prominent German writers and intellectuals, such as Bertolt Brecht (left) and Johannes Becher, championed the East German communist system against West German capitalism. They accepted the restrictions on freedom in the GDR as a necessary temporary expedient on the road to building a better society.

RIGHT: A poorly armed demonstrator assails a Soviet tank on Pots-damerplatz during the workers' uprising of June 17 1953. Starting with unrest over pay and working hours, the revolt opened out into demands for fundamental democratic freedoms.

being increased by 10 percent with no rise in pay. With this last blow, discontent over-flowed on to the streets.

When the announcement was made, workers were engaged on a major construction project near the center of East Berlin, building Stalinallee (later renamed Karl-Marx-Allee), a showpiece avenue of ornately decorative apartment blocks in the Stalinist style (known to Berliners as 'cake-icing' architecture). The workers downed tools and headed for the center of govern-

ment on Leipzigerstrasse. Their numbers swelled by sympathetic passers-by who joined in, about 8000 protesters swarmed in front of the House of Ministeries, demanding to speak to government leaders. They were promised that the rise in work norms would be rescinded, but this gesture came too late. A call was launched for a general strike and Western radio stations broadcast this appeal across the length and breadth of East Germany. Demands emerged for free elections and the reunification of Germany.

RIGHT: While the rioting raged on June 17 in East Berlin, Soviet armor took up positions on the sector border to deter West Berliners from joining in. Many Berliners were angered that the Western occupying powers took no action to support the uprising in the East.

On the following morning, June 17, more than 300,000 workers responded to the strike call. In East Berlin an estimated 100,000 demonstrators marched on the House of Ministries. Helpless to control the situation, the GDR leadership called for support from the Soviet Army. General Pavel Dibrova, the Soviet commander, declared martial law and ordered his troops, tanks and armored cars into the crowded Leipzigerstrasse. The demonstrators responded to gunfire with bricks and bottles, and fighting spread in scattered skirmishes through East Berlin. By nightfall the Soviet army had restored government control.

What exactly occurred, beyond these bare bones of the event, on that dramatic, chaotic day is still hard to establish. Some East German sources put the number of deaths at only 21, with a further seven subsequently executed for their part in the uprising. A reporter for the British newspaper *The Guardian* wrote immediately after the event:

The Red Army troops evidently were given the strictest instructions to behave with restraint. There are few cases reported of their having opened fire on demonstrators – even though they were stoned and insulted and their tanks and armoured cars physically attacked by the demonstrators.

According to other accounts, however,

LEFT: The order from the Soviet military authorities declaring a state of emergency in East Berlin from 1pm on June 17 1953. Issued in the name of the Soviet military commander in Berlin, General Pavel Dibrova, the order banned all demonstrations and instituted a curfew for the hours of darkness.

the Soviets were responsible for a massacre on a far larger scale, shooting several hundred rioters and executing another 92 civilians in the immediate aftermath of the fighting. A number of East German policemen and Soviet soldiers were also executed for siding with the demonstrators or refusing to fire on them.

LEFT: Demonstrators on Potsdamerplatz scatter as Soviet tanks advance up the street. There are wildly conflicting estimates of the number of people killed or injured in the fighting.

Whatever the scale of the events, their impact was decisive. The communist leadership tried to blur the significance of the uprising by claiming, probably with a grain of truth, that Western agents and ex-Nazis had exploited the workers' genuine grievances, transforming a legitimate protest into an attempt to overthrow the communist system. But nothing could hide the unpopularity of the communist regime: in the wake of the June uprising, one communist leader estimated that the system enjoyed the support of only one in ten East Germans. When the communist-controled Writers' Union, standing reality on its head, declared that the government had lost confidence in the people, Bertolt Brecht, who had publicly approved the repression of June 17, privately wrote his bitter satirical poem *The Solution*. If the people had lost the government's confidence, asked the poet:

Would it not then
be simpler for the government
to dissolve the people
and elect another?

The uprising had laid bare the realities of power in East Germany. The regime did not stand firm on any rock of popular support; it

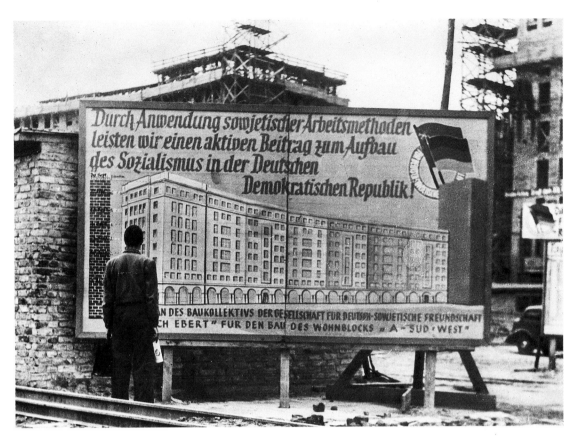

was an unstable structure propped up by the strength of the Soviet army. The communist system had been imposed on a reluctant population by an occupying army and was sustained by the will of Moscow. If Moscow ever decided to pull away the props, the whole edifice would crumble in a cloud of dust.

J W STALIN

2
CAPITAL OF
THE COLD WAR

LEFT: Members of the East German youth movement, Freie Deutsche Jugend, pose with a portrait of Stalin in the summer of 1951. The youth movement was dedicated to creating a new generation of Germans with communist attitudes and ideals.

In Heinrich Böll's story *Business is Business*, written in the early years of the West German economic miracle, the narrator looks back nostalgically on the days of the black market as a time of relative decency and friendliness. With a black marketeer, he claims, 'we used to chat sometimes about hunger and the war; and he would sometimes give me a cigarette if I was broke'. Now the same man has gone legal and chases away a ragged urchin who doesn't quite have the money to buy some sweets. 'I liked it better before,' the narrator concludes, 'when he didn't need to drive someone away who was short of five pfennigs; but now he's got a real business, and business is business'.

In the 1950s the new Federal Republic, built on the ruins of Hitler's Germany, was not an especially charitable or comradely place. But few of its citizens shared Böll's doubts about the direction of their society, bowled over as they were by the pace of economic recovery and the neon-lit perspectives of a consumer paradise. Between 1948 and 1964, to take one measure of West German resurgence, industrial output increased by 600 percent. On all the graphs, population, income, car ownership, GNP, the lines climbed resolutely upward. In West Berlin, hampered by its bizarre and precarious political situation, the effects of the economic miracle were less marked, but they were still sufficient to contrast flagrantly with the East.

When journalist Norman Gelb took up residence in Berlin in 1960, he noted that, although the city 'remained a single geographical entity' with no Wall dividing East from West, it was already 'far more conspicuously bisected' than any city he had ever visited before. West Berlin, as Gelb later wrote in his book *The Berlin Wall*, was 'a bustling place, very much on the move, very much up-to-date', the rubble of war mostly tidied away, the Kurfürstendamm lined with 'elegant shops flaunting the latest fashions and chic travel goods', the nightclubs and cabarets awakening echos of the 1920s, when Berlin had been the capital of European decadence. By contrast, East Berlin struck the newcomer as 'unmistakably someplace else . . . drowsy and old-fashioned, a touch Ruritanian'; weed-grown bombsites and rusting girders scarred the Mitte, the historic center of the city, where men and women 'dowdily attired but not undignified' moved without bustle or haste between buildings still pock-marked by the bullets and shrapnel of 1945.

The urgent exhortations of the massive Communist street placards – Build the Socialist Fatherland for Peace and Progress – were the only visible sign of direction, and they seemed ironic rather than purposeful.

There were many reasons for the failure of the East German economic recovery to match that in the West, including the clumsiness of centralized planning, the false

RIGHT: Massed ranks of East Germans, mostly armed militiamen, assemble in Marx-Engels Platz, East Berlin, in May 1955, to celebrate the tenth anniversary of the 'liberation' of the country by Soviet forces.

priorities of heavy industrialization, and the lack of American capital for investment. Even after the Soviet Union ended direct confiscation of output as reparations in 1954, unfavorable trade agreements imposed by Moscow leeched off East German wealth for the benefit of the more backward Soviet economy. With every year that passed, standards of living in the two Germanies drew further apart.

The division of Germany was formalized in May 1955, when the United States, Britain and France granted the Federal Republic full independence; the Soviets responded by declaring the GDR a sovereign state. Both Germanies were remilitarized, the Federal Republic within the Nato alliance and the GDR in the Warsaw Pact. Relations between the two states were blankly hostile. According to the so-called 'Hallstein doctrine', the Federal Republic refused to recognize the existence of the GDR, and would not establish diplomatic relations with any other country that recognized the GDR. As far as the Bonn government was concerned, every citizen of the GDR was rightfully a citizen of a united Germany (a Germany which, in the view of Bonn, included about one third of postwar Poland).

The hardening of the Cold War division of Europe in the 1950s and the lack of any relationship between East and West Germany made the already anomalous position of Berlin even more incongruous. It is easily forgotten that the Berlin Wall, when it came,

ABOVE: In 1953 the East German authorities cut the tram routes between East and West Berlin; new lines had to be laid to make routes that did not cross the border. It was a small step toward the eventual partition of the city.

LEFT: An American soldier eats with a West Berlin family who have invited him into their home. Although there were always tensions between the forces of the Western Allies and the Berlin population, they were much better liked than were the Soviet troops in East Berlin.

RIGHT: A demonstration in
East Berlin in 1952
commemorates the
Soviet October
Revolution. The endless
reiteration of pro-Soviet
propaganda and the
virtually enforced
attendance at meetings,
marches and parades to
show 'socialist solidarity'
did much to alienate the
population from the East
German regime.

RIGHT: A demonstration in
East Berlin in 1952
commemorates the
Soviet October
Revolution. The endless
reiteration of pro-Soviet
propaganda and the
virtually enforced
attendance at meetings,
marches and parades to
show 'socialist solidarity'
did much to alienate the
population from the East
German regime.

was only the last brick in a fortified line stretching from the Baltic to the Black Sea. Barbed wire, minefields, armed guards, dogs and watchtowers fenced off the people of Eastern Europe from the West along the borders of all the communist states, including East Germany. The rest of this more extended Wall was in place by 1953. Only in Berlin was there virtually free passage between East and West. In 1952 the communists had blocked some streets leading from East Berlin into the West and had cut off bus and tram services between the two halves of the city, but 66 pedestrian and 22 vehicle crossing points remained open, subject to little more than perfunctory surveillance by border guards whose main interest was stopping the import of banned goods into the East.

Thousands of local people streamed back and forth across the border in the course of their everyday lives. About 60,000 who lived in the East, where subsidized accommodation, transport and food made life cheap, worked in the West, to be paid at the higher western wage levels. Easterners crossed into the West for entertainment at cinemas showing Hollywood films – there were special cut-price movie theaters near the sector borders – and Westerners went to the East to purchase cheap food and drink, despite exhortations from the West Berlin authorities to spend their money at home rather than contribute to the communist economy. Trains on the urban rail network, the *U-bahn* (underground railway) and the

S-bahn (elevated railway), ran on routes that took in both East and West Berlin. The *S-bahn*, much used by West Berlin commuters, was run by the East German Deutsche Reichsbahn. In many places the East-West border ran almost unnoticed through local communities, and was crossed without thinking every time a resident went to his nearest shop or visited his neighbors across the street.

Free movement between the different sectors of the city was guaranteed by the four-power Potsdam Agreement, which still officially regulated the running of Berlin even after East and West Germany gained their formal independence. In the rest of the Federal Republic the British, French and American occupying armies had been transmuted into Germany's military allies, operating alongside their German colleagues for the defense of Europe. But in Berlin the wartime Allies retained many of the rights of conquerors. Although West Berlin was acknowledged as adhering to the Federal Republic, it could only send deputies to the Bundestag in Bonn in a non-voting capacity. The Federal Republic was not permitted to station military forces in Berlin, to conscript Berliners into the armed forces, or even to manufacture arms in Berlin factories. The air routes into the city remained under Allied military air-traffic control and Lufthansa, the West German airline, was not allowed to fly there. The powers of the Allied military commanders in the city were substantial on paper, and

LEFT: Girls in the communist youth organization display their disciplined movement at an official spectacle in 1954. The tone of East German society was meant to be clean and wholesome, in self-conscious contrast to the decadent West.

occasionally exercised in practice. No citizen of Berlin was permitted to own a weapon – even the possession of kitchen knives was theoretically counter to the military law – and political demonstrations had to be authorized by the commander in the relevant sector.

Officially the same occupation statute applied to East Berlin, but the Soviets allowed East Germany to claim the city as its capital and even permitted East German armed forces into Berlin on special occasions for military parades, although the Western occupation forces would have been within their rights if they had arrested any East German soldier setting foot in the city. All four occupying powers claimed the right of access to the whole of the city, East

LEFT: Units of the Volkspolizei, the East German People's Police, popularly known as the 'Vopos', head for a parade in Marx-Engels Platz.

ABOVE: The East German government established armed works' militias based on factories and offices, ostensibly to defend economic installations against saboteurs. The militias were another element in the constant pressure toward group, as opposed to private, activity. They also provided a large body of armed men at the service of the state in case of need.

pounds. A few dollars were enough to make many of the boys change sides between cups of coffee.

Any East Germans visiting West Berlin for a beer or a trip to the cinema might be approached by a stranger who would ask them if they wanted to earn a little pocket money by carrying secret letters to the East or reporting on Soviet troop movements. One agent, Werner Moch, calculated that he had been personally responsible for re-cruiting more than 35 people in this casual way. The number of individuals earning a living from espionage in Berlin in the late 1950s has been variously estimated at be-tween 7000 and 12,000.

The number of espionage agencies oper-ating in the city was equally extraordinary. On the Eastern side spying had been nationalized – all espionage and counter-espionage operations were in the hands of the Stasi and the KGB. But in the West private enterprise flourished. Alongside the foreign heavyweights – the American CIA, the British SIS and the French SDECE – a jumbled underworld of West German spy firms competed for business, entrepreneurs selling secrets and subversion in a free mar-ket. Their customers were chiefly the foreign intelligence agencies and West Ger-man political parties or pressure groups. Any business in West Berlin, from an insur-ance company to a clothes shop, was likely to be a front for espionage. Inevitably, many operators in this shadowy area were tempted to make their profits dishonestly. Some made up the secrets they sold, attri-buting them to non-existent sources; others sold their services to both sides, without owing allegiance to either.

The most successful, and most contro-versial, of the West German intelligence organizations was unquestionably that established by General Reinhard Gehlen, who had been an intelligence chief on the Eastern front during Hitler's war. Initially a private venture funded by the CIA, which was quite prepared to overlook Gehlen's past Nazi connections, the 'Org' eventually transmuted into an official West German state intelligence agency, the Bundes-nachrichtendienst (BND), directly answer-able to Hans Globke, Adenauer's state secretary, who also had past Nazi associa-tions. Gehlen operated extensive surveil-lance of left-wing groups in West Germany, indiscriminately identified as 'subversive', leading to accusations of the covert reintro-duction of a police state. However contro-versial his role in West German internal politics, Gehlen could claim substantial

and West. Soviet military patrols regularly toured West Berlin and the Western Allies all sent 'flag-waving' patrols into the East.

The openness of the border in the 1950s made Berlin a notorious hotbed of espion-age. Nowhere else in the world was it so easy for the agents of hostile secret services to meet and do deals, or for corrupt officials from either side to contact a customer wish-ing to buy their secrets. The city seethed with informers, double and triple agents, spies and spymasters. A former Austrian in-telligence officer, writing under the pseudo-nym E H Cookridge, described the Café Warsaw in East Berlin as:

A sort of Stock Exchange for secrets, with half the tables taken up by Soviet, Czech, Polish, British, American, French and East and West German agents. The going rate for a scrap of negotiable information could fall as low as five success in foreign espionage in the early 1950s. Exploiting the deep disillusionment of many East Germans with their own state system, Gehlen was able to recruit agents from minor officials in the communist bureaucracy up to the highest levels of the GDR administration, including the country's vice-president, Hermann Kastner. All the threads of Gehlen's organization, which stretched out to agents as far east as Moscow, led back to offices in West Berlin.

The ease of transit between the communist and capitalist worlds in Berlin, which so facilitated Gehlen's operations, had its hazards for the intelligence community as well as its advantages. Kidnapping was an ever-present threat: through the 1950s, there were more than 200 cases of agents or defectors abducted from West Berlin by the Stasi. In February 1953 one of Gehlen's leading operatives, Major Wolfgang Hoher, had a drug slipped into his drink in a West Berlin bar and woke up in the hands of Stasi interrogators in the East. Even more damaging was the very similar disappearance of Otto John, the head of the West German government's counter-espionage organization, the Federal Internal Security Office. On the night of July 20 1954, John went drinking in West Berlin with Wolfgang Wolgemuth, a doctor who was in the pay of the KGB. Either drugged or dead drunk, John allowed Wolgemuth to take him into East Berlin, where he was incarcerated in a Soviet 'safe house' in the Karlshorst district. That, at least, is the most probable version of the story; Gehlen always believed that John had been a double agent and had defected, using the alleged kidnapping as a cover to maintain his credibility in the West.

ABOVE: In 1953 this statue of Stalin stood in Unter den Linden. The quote from the Soviet dictator alongside the statue reads: 'Long live peace between the nations.'

The prevalence of double agents was a notable feature of the Berlin espionage scene. Since the intelligence agencies on both sides were staffed by men of the same nationality and background, it was very easy to infiltrate an agent into your enemy's organization or to persuade one of the opposition to engage in a double-cross. The sheer closeness of contact encouraged waverings of allegiance and facilitated recruitment by both sides. Gehlen's organization was severely damaged when Hans Joachim Geyer, one of its leading desk officers in West Berlin, allowed himself to be recruited by the East Germans. For most of 1953 Geyer passed on to the communists microfilm copies of every document that passed through his hands. Once his cover was blown he simply decamped to safety in East Berlin, a journey of only a few minutes.

LEFT: Dr Otto John, the head of West Germany counter-intelligence, appears at a press conference in East Berlin in 1955 after having fallen into the hands of the Stasi. John publicly denounced Western intelligence, but later returned to the West and claimed he had acted under duress.

many had upset traditional notions of patriotism and treachery. Gehlen and John, for example, hated and distrusted one another because John had participated in the German officers' conspiracy to assassinate Hitler in 1944, while Gehlen had remained faithful to his Nazi masters and had shown a marked readiness to employ old SS operatives in his postwar spy organization. Gehlen had cause to recognize the unreliability of ex-Nazis as employees in 1961, when it was revealed that one of his most trusted associates, ex-SS officer Heinz Felfe, had been spying for the Soviet Union for ten years.

The successive heads of the Stasi in the 1950s, Wilhelm Zaisser, Ernst Wollweber and Erich Mielke, were all Stalinists with impeccable anti-Nazi records: Wollweber, for example, had been arrested in Sweden during the war for sabotaging ore shipments to Germany. But they all employed ex-Nazi Gestapo and intelligence officers in the ranks of the Stasi after 're-education'. Although professing an implacable ideological hostility, the staff of East and West German secret organizations were easily interchangeable.

In this fog of cynicism and conflicting loyalties, the British and American intelligence agencies were often lost and hopelessly vulnerable. The CIA's first major venture in Berlin was a campaign of sabotage at the start of the 1950s. These were the days when the United States was committed to

ABOVE: Two East Berlin workers and their wives return from a ceremony at which the men have been decorated for their contribution to building socialism. The GDR depended on moral exhortation rather than material incentives to encourage increased output.

RIGHT: The kidnapping of East German lawyer Dr Walter Linse in West Berlin and his abduction to the East in July 1952 caused a storm of protest. Together with other lawyers and jurists in East Germany, Linse had founded the Investigation Committee of Free Jurists to publicize cases of political oppression; the resulting persecution caused him to flee to West Berlin. What happened to him after his abduction is unknown.

Although mercenary motives explained many betrayals, the swift transition from Naziism to Cold War confrontation in Ger-

BELOW: A door in the spy tunnel, built by the CIA and SIS under the Soviet sector of Berlin, bears signs purporting to bar entry on the authority of the Soviet high command. These signs were placed there by Western intelligence in the hope of deterring anyone who might chance upon the tunnel from the East.

'rolling back communism', and when many CIA officers were still obsessed by the memory of World War II operations behind enemy lines in occupied Europe. They took over financing and organization of the Kampfgruppe gegen Unmenschlichkeit (KgU), an anti-communist network with excellent contacts throughout East Germany, and set it to the task of blowing up bridges, railway lines and electricity pylons. This campaign successfully exacerbated relations between East and West, but was otherwise a fiasco. Hundreds of East Germans were arrested as the Stasi scooped up whole sections of the KgU in a series of coordinated police raids. By the spring of 1952, almost all the organization's leaders were in prison and many anti-communists who had wanted no part in sabotage had suffered the same fate.

In the mid-1950s, Western intelligence seemed to have compensated for this disaster with the success of Operation Gold, the famous Berlin tunnel, one of the largest and boldest espionage efforts ever mounted by the SIS and the CIA. Starting in the suburb of Rudow, inside the American-controled sector of West Berlin, US army engineers dug a tunnel one third of a mile long, stretching under the border to Alte Gleinicke in East Berlin; the work was plausibly disguised as the building of a top-secret radar station. Nicknamed 'Harvey's Hole' after the CIA's Berlin station chief Bill Harvey, the tunnel was planned to cut across the line of underground telephone

RIGHT: The Berlin spy tunnel was packed with the most sophisticated equipment available at the time for eaves-dropping on the many thousand telephone calls passing between East Berlin and the cities of eastern Europe and the Soviet Union. The tunnel cost around $25 million to construct and equip.

cables linking East Berlin with Eastern Europe and the Soviet Union. The site of these cables had been identified by an anti-communist East German telephone employee recruited by Gehlen's 'Org'.

Once the tunnel was completed British Post Office engineers went underground and applied taps to the cables, allowing the British and the Americans to tape all telephone communications flowing eastward out of Berlin, including those from the Soviet military headquarters and embassy. Operation Gold cost around 25 million dollars but it seemed cheap at the price. From April 1955 a flood of uncoded Soviet communications began pouring through to Western

RIGHT: An East German Vopo trains his binoculars on a radar station in the American sector of Berlin. Construction work at the radar station was used as cover for the building of the tunnel.

intelligence, such a quantity of material that an army of Russian emigrés had to be recruited full-time to transcribe the tapes when they were flown back to London and Washington.

When Soviet security officers broke into the east end of the tunnel in April 1956 and exposed the operation to the world's press – adopting a hypocritical tone of righteous indignation – Western intelligence chiefs assumed that the operation had been uncovered by an accident of surveillance. The massive task of transcribing and analyzing the tapes already recorded continued for the next five years. Despite its premature end, the operation was considered a major success.

Unfortunately for the West, however, one SIS intelligence officer who had known the secret of the tunnel was a Soviet double agent, George Blake. The story of Blake's activities in Berlin is typical of the complex, tortuous espionage game being played out in the city at the heart of the Cold War. Soon after taking up his post in the SIS station at the Olympia Stadium complex, Blake informed station chief Peter Lunn that the Soviets were keen to recruit him as a double agent. He suggested that he should be authorized to pretend to go along with the deal, passing over a trickle of trivial or false secrets to his Soviet controller, in return for which he hoped to glean genuine information on the Soviet intelligence network. SIS agreed to the plan with enthusiasm. So a bizarrely complex pattern of betrayal was woven: SIS thought Blake was pretending to be a double agent in a game they controled, whereas he really was a double agent in a game controled by the KGB. This arrangement had great advantages for Blake. He could openly admit to covert contacts with the Russians as part of the SIS deception plan. The KGB would feed him with the odd piece of information, the name of a minor agent whose usefulness was exhausted, for example, that he could pass on to his SIS masters, keeping his reputation high. Meanwhile, he was providing the Soviets with every valuable document that came into his hands at the Olympia Stadium. Blake gave the communists lists of agents working for SIS in Eastern Europe; he revealed the whereabouts of a high-ranking East German defector, Robert Bialek, who was then abducted from West Berlin by the KGB and shot; and he was able to tell the Soviets that one of their own military intelligence officers, Lieutenant-Colonel Peter Popov, was secretly working for the Americans. Blake also, of course, informed the Soviets about the tunnel. It was not until

1961 that, with the unmasking of Blake as a double agent, the total failure of the tunnel project became apparent. Since he had unquestionably told the Soviets about it from the start, they must have ensured that no genuinely secret material was transmitted by the tapped landlines, while at the same time 'planting' phony secrets to mislead Western intelligence. Blake had ensured that the tunnel would be not just a waste of time and money for the West, but a positive contribution to the Soviet campaign of disinformation and manipulation.

Despite these Western failures, the problem of espionage seriously worried the East German leadership, obsessed as they were by internal security, and made them long for some solution to the Berlin situation that would stitch up this only remaining tear in the Iron Curtain. But the most urgent problem for Ulbricht and his colleagues was emigration. Like all countries in the communist bloc, East Germany had taken extreme

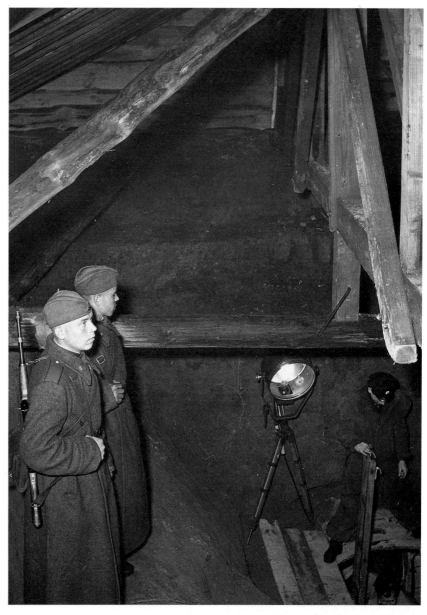

BELOW: East German soldiers guard the point at which the communists broke into the tunnel. Western intelligence believed the tunnel had been discovered by chance, but its existence had in fact been revealed to the Soviets by British double agent George Blake.

measures to prevent its citizens from traveling to the West. The fortified border that stretched from the Baltic to Czechoslovakia was designed to keep East Germans in, as much as to keep Westerners out. Only the most privileged and trusted individuals could ever obtain a visa to visit the capitalist world, and even then they were shadowed by Stasi agents.

But with virtual free passage from East to West Berlin, any East German who wished to emigrate to the Federal Republic had only to walk across into the welcoming arms of the Western authorities. The emigrants were housed in a temporary reception center at Marienfelde, interrogated by counter-intelligence officers and then, if they wished, flown out to West Germany. They were accorded immediate citizenship of the Federal Republic with full rights and benefits and if they were classified as 'political refugees', as almost all were, they were given official help to establish themselves with a job and accommodation. Since the economy was booming and unemployment almost non-existent, integration in a new life in the West usually posed no formidable problems.

Through the 1950s, East German emigrants filed across the Berlin border at a rate of around 20,000 a month, a total of two and a half million people in the decade, about one in seven of the entire East German population. They came from all walks of life, from agricultural workers to surgeons, but

there was a preponderance of the young – almost half were under 25 – and the skilled. By the end of the decade it was almost impossible to find a plumber or an electrician in East Germany; universities, schools and hospitals were depleted of staff; factories ran short of engineers. The cumulative impact on the economy was catastrophic. In a vain attempt to stem the hemorrhage, the East German government introduced legislation in 1957 making *Republikflucht* – fleeing the country – a criminal offence. But they had no way of enforcing this law.

The reasons for this mass emigration were as complex as those for any of the other great population movements of modern times; that of Asians from the Indian sub-continent to Britain, for example, or of Mexicans into the United States. A dynamic, rapidly expanding economy will always tend to suck in labor from more impoverished states within its sphere of influence. The Federal Republic was drawing in workers from as far afield as Portugal, Yugoslavia and Turkey; there were to be over four million of these immigrants in West Germany by the 1980s. In one sense, the immigration from the East was only an aspect of this wider flow of labor from areas of poverty and unemployment toward sources of wealth and jobs. Some of the reasons given by East Germans for emigrating were almost identical to those that might be expressed, for instance, by British emigrants to Canada or Australia. West

OPPOSITE: East Germans fleeing to the West queue outside a West Berlin center for refugees in 1953. Their faces have been whited out on the photograph to prevent them being identified by the East German authorities.

LEFT: A center for refugees run by the Red Cross in Charlottenburg, West Berlin. About 2.5 million East Germans emigrated to West Germany in the 1950s.

Germany was a land of opportunity, offering prospects for material self-improvement, better housing, an escape route for the ambitious from the restrictions of a more stagnant economy and a less open society.

But the motivation of the millions deserting the East could by no means be reduced to a simple question of economics. Indeed, the standard of living in East Germany was showing a marked improvement by the end of the 1950s, although lagging far behind the West. Accommodation was generally of poor quality; most families lived in cramped apartments with few facilities in charmless new blocks, but rents were heavily subsidized and thus easily affordable by all. Similarly, food may have been of poor quality and supplies uncertain but at least it was cheap and no one starved. The basics of an effective welfare state were in place; it was as rare to see someone with inadequate clothing as to spot a person dressed with notable style.

The economic grievances expressed by East Germans were inextricably bound up with politics. The communist regime had, in essence, succeeded in maintaining permanent wartime conditions in the East, which is why the country so often gave visitors from the West the impression of traveling

back in time to the 1940s. There was the same rationing and queueing as in wartime, the same poor quality of food, and the sudden inexplicable shortages of essential items: one moment it was potatoes, then soap, then razorblades. There was the indefinable air of drabness, like a thin layer of gray dust, that seemed to settle on everything and everybody. There was the obsession with security and unity. And there were the endless exhortations to greater effort in the collective struggle, the cultivation of a public tone of high-mindedness and self-sacrifice, now in the struggle to build socialism rather than the struggle to win the war for the Fatherland, but otherwise indistinguishable from the rhetoric-saturated atmosphere of World War II.

East Germany was a vast school in which the lessons of Marxist politics were being taught every day by rote to classes of mostly recalcitrant pupils. The population resented being constantly reminded of the evils of Germany's recent past – Brecht once commented that free elections were impossible in East Germany because the people would re-elect the Nazis – and loathed the endless ritual praises chanted to the Glorious Soviet Union. At the obligatory works' meetings to pass motions in support of the Party leadership, it was difficult safely to remain silent and non-committal, and impossible if you wanted promotion. Enforced conformity bred cynicism and self-loathing.

Most hated were the Stasi, the secret service whose tentacles reached out into the most remote corners of East German life. As well as the official 'commissioners' that the Stasi maintained quite openly in every major factory or agricultural collective, there was an ever-expanding army of secret informers who kept watch on colleagues and acquaintances, reporting back on those who privately criticized the regime, grumbled about shortages, or talked of emigration. To refuse to inform, if asked, would damage your prospects and those of your children. Every East German learnt to be cautious in expressing any opinion or attitude that might cause trouble if passed on to the authorities.

Even among that minority of the population more or less committed to 'building socialism', there was much discontent and disquiet with the direction pursued by Ulbricht and his colleagues. In the aftermath of Nikita Khrushchev's denunciation of Stalin in 1956 and the Polish and Hungarian uprisings of the same year, there was a move through most of Eastern Europe to 'de-Stalinize' the communist regimes. This brought to power new communist leaders such as Janos Kadar in Hungary and Wladyslaw Gomulka in Poland, who strove to construct a popular base for their governments through a small measure of liberalization and a larger dose of nationalism. In East Germany, however, Ulbricht and his

fellow Stalinists kept firm control and slapped down any calls for reform. In 1957 Wolfgang Harich, a communist academic teaching at Humboldt University in East Berlin, was sentenced to ten years' imprisonment for advocating the abolition of the secret police, a genuine choice of candidates in elections, freedom for the churches and universities and an end to the collectivization of agriculture.

To the long list of reasons for emigrating from the GDR – career prospects blocked because of known involvement in the Church or expression of non-conformist views; frustration at the promotion of a less talented fellow worker who toed the Party line; outrage at the obtuseness of bureaucratic managers; rejection of enforced participation in demonstrations and meetings; desire for a better standard of living; longing for travel, excitement and adventure; nausea provoked by the endless parroting of Marxist cliché; hatred and fear of the secret police; the wish to be free to speak one's mind – another pressing motive was added at the end of the 1950s: the widespread fear that a swift move by the Soviets might at any moment shut off West Berlin and leave the East Germans trapped behind the uncrossable barrier of the Iron Curtain. The prolonged crisis that was to culminate in the building of the Berlin Wall began with a speech by Khrushchev on November 10 1958. The Soviet leader called on the Western powers to abandon 'the occupation

regime in Berlin, thus facilitating the normalization of the situation in the capital of the GDR'. A fortnight later, he followed this up with an ultimatum: if the West did not withdraw its garrisons within six months, the Soviet Union would unilaterally declare Berlin a 'free city' and hand over all responsibility to the East Germans, including control of access routes to West Berlin by land and air. As a sovereign state, East Germany would have the right to deny foreigners permission to travel across its territory. Khrushchev's ultimatum in practice threatened a renewal of the Berlin blockade. When the Western Allies refused to budge, the Soviet leader quietly allowed the six-month deadline to elapse without carrying out his threat. But the question of Berlin had been placed back at the top of the Cold War agenda.

A mercurial, restless, flamboyant personality, Khrushchev instinctively made use of gesture and provocation in his approach to foreign policy. He was convinced that communism would win the Cold War and had no desire to cause a hot war, which he realistically estimated no one would win – 'after a nuclear war', Khrushchev once said, 'the living will envy the dead'. But he was prepared to press on any weak point in the capitalist structure to score prestige points and perhaps gain a little ground. Berlin was ideal for his purposes. With his taste for earthy metaphors, Khrushchev once described the city as 'the testicles of the

LEFT: Ulbricht had aged dramatically by the time this jovial photo was taken of him, bespectacled and gray-bearded, with Nikita Khrushchev in 1963. He was 81 years old before he was finally prised out of office in 1971.

West – when I want the West to scream, I squeeze on Berlin'.

In retrospect, the whole diplomatic game which built to the climactic crisis of 1961 can be seen to have involved a large element of shadow-boxing. Both the Soviets and the Western Allies had in principle been seeking a peace agreement with a reunited Germany ever since the end of World War II. But in practice they had long settled for cultivating the independence of their separate halves of the former German state. Even the West German government, although overtly committed to the sacred cause of reunification, had settled comfortably into membership of Nato and into ruling the lion's share of the German population and economy. Similarly, all parties deplored a divided Berlin but all parties were used to it. For the Soviets, the situation was irritating but ultimately tolerable. For the Western powers, and even for the West German government under Adenauer, it sometimes seemed, West Berlin was an unwelcome liability but one of which they could not divest themselves. Behind the Soviet rhetoric of anti-imperialism and the western rhetoric of freedom, there was no adequate will to change the status quo.

The one player in the game who truly needed something to change was the East German government. The continued existence of West Berlin was an affront to East German claims of sovereign independence; what independent country could tolerate

the permanent occupation of half its capital city by its declared enemies? And, above all, the flood of emigrants to the West threatened the collapse of the East German economic and social infrastructure. Ulbricht put what pressure he could on Khrushchev to take action, but Khrushchev would only threaten the West; if his bluff was called, in the end he would go no further.

BELOW: Willy Brandt (center right), the mayor of West Berlin, shows an American visitor, Senator Hubert Humphrey of Minnesota, around the city. A worthy successor to Ernst Reuter, Brandt displayed a vision that was eventually to transform relations between East and West Germany.

RIGHT: The sudden closing of the border between East and West Berlin in August 1961 created some bizarre anomalies. This German boy lived in Eiskeller, which belonged to the British sector but was an enclave inside the territory of the Soviet sector. When the Vopos threatened to stop the child cycling from Eiskeller to his school in West Berlin, the British military authorities provided him with an armed escort every day, until the point was made.

A worsening both of superpower relations and of East Germany's refugee problem finally precipitated the Berlin crisis in 1961. The start of the year saw the advent in the White House of a new President, John F Kennedy. Khrushchev viewed Kennedy as inexperienced and possibly responsive to pressure, especially after the mishandling of the Bay of Pigs landings in Cuba in April. The Soviet Union was in bullish mood because of its lead over the United States in the space race, and it was under pressure to assert its prestige in the communist world as the Chinese mounted their campaign against Moscow 'revisionists'. Altogether, the moment seemed opportune for Khrushchev to confront Kennedy over Berlin.

When the two leaders met for a summit conference in Vienna at the start of June, Khrushchev suddenly rounded on the President after an amicable first day of talks, demanding a Western withdrawal from Berlin within six months and threatening that a refusal could lead to war. This aggressive rant left Kennedy visibly shocked and disturbed, a reaction which convinced Khrushchev the pressure was worth keeping up. The US President and his advisers left Vienna almost believing Khrushchev might be mad enough to precipitate war over Berlin. A Berlin Task Force was set up in Washington to monitor the situation, while bellicose pronouncements continued to flow from Moscow. Old plans from 1948 were revived for an armored column to drive through to West Berlin if the Soviet Union imposed a new blockade.

Meanwhile there had been a further sharp increase in the level of emigration from East Germany. Uncertainties about the future, the diplomatic crisis, and an economic downturn with worsening food shortages and increased 'work norms', drove more and more Easterners to seek refuge in the West. The East German authorities responded aggressively, drafting in squads of Vopos (People's Police) to check on road and rail travelers heading into Berlin, and detain those suspected of intending to cross to the West; anyone carrying a Bible in their luggage was turned back as suspect. New restrictions were imposed on easterners with jobs in West Berlin and they were pressured to take up employment in the East, where emigration had created hundreds of thousands of vacancies in the labor market. This crackdown only added fuel to the mounting panic provoked by the hostile pronouncements of communist politicians. Everyone believed something decisive would happen soon, and many wanted to get out of East Germany before it did. Over the weekend of Easter 1961, 3000 people fled to the West in four days. By July emigration had topped 30,000 a month; the normal reception centers in West Berlin had been augmented by a series of temporary camps but even these were overflowing. Special flights shifted the emigrants on to West Germany as fast as they could be processed. If

LEFT: The newly
constructed Wall at
Charlottenstrasse in mid-
August 1961; it has not
yet been topped with
barbed wire. US soldiers
had no orders to
intervene and stood by
powerless while the city
was divided.

this rate of emigration continued, the East German economy would collapse.

An obvious solution to the crisis had already occurred to the chairman of the US Senate Foreign Relations Committee, Senator William Fulbright: 'I don't understand why the East Germans don't close their border, because I think they have a right to close it.' In fact, under the Potsdam agreement they had no such right in Berlin – but Potsdam was a dead letter. As early as 1958 the East German leadership had considered a contingency plan for a fence around West Berlin, and in March 1961 Ulbricht obtained agreement from a Warsaw Pact meeting to begin preparations for such a move in earnest, in case no other solution could be found. The member of the SED central committee put in charge of the job was the future East German leader, Erich Honecker. The planning and assembly of materials proceeded in great secrecy. On June 15, at a rare press conference, Ulbricht sought to scotch rumors with a straight denial: 'The construction workers of our capital are for the most part busy building apartment houses, and their working capacities are fully employed to that end,' he declared. 'Nobody intends to put up a wall.'

Ulbricht would have preferred the Soviet Union to take positive action to drive the Western garrisons out of West Berlin, but for all his bombastic talk Khrushchev was not prepared to act. The Soviet leader and his diplomatic representatives had spent much of the summer explaining to Western leaders just how easily the Soviet nuclear arsenal could destroy their countries if they resisted over Berlin. But by the beginning of August, Khrushchev knew the United States was ready to call his bluff.

On July 25, hoping to leave the Soviets in no doubt of the United States' determination to hold its ground, Kennedy had addressed the American people in the gravest terms, declaring West Berlin 'the great testing place of Western courage and will' and asserting his readiness 'to resist with force, if force is used upon us'. The President announced his intention to increase the military budget, call up 250,000 reservists and step up the civil defense program to provide nuclear shelters in case of war. Khrushchev might have been tempted to dismiss such fighting talk as a counter-bluff by the United States; that he did not was a tribute to the virtues of leaky Western security. Fortunately for the cause of peace, the higher levels of Nato were riddled with Soviet spies, who confirmed to Moscow that the intransigent Western response was genuine: the West was no more prepared to withdraw from Berlin under threat in 1961 than it had been in 1948. If Khrushchev insisted on taking unilateral action, Nato would respond with force if necessary. Knowing this, and not wanting to fight a war over Berlin, the Soviet leader forced Ulbricht to carry out an East German solution to the emigration crisis.

RIGHT: In the semi-rural outlying suburbs of Berlin, as at this campsite in Kladow, the border remained unfenced for a brief period after the center of the city was sealed.

The atmosphere in West Berlin at the beginning of August 1961 was outwardly calm, but with an inevitable undercurrent of tension and unease. A steady trickle of wealthier Berliners were withdrawing to the greater security of West Germany; real estate prices fell fast as abandoned properties came on the market. Even if few citizens expected a full-scale communist takeover, West Berliners feared a deal might be struck with the Soviets that would compromise their rights. The city's Social Democrat mayor, Willy Brandt, insisted in talks with Adenauer and with Western leaders that the integrity of West Berlin should on no account be sacrificed to expediency.

In fact, Brandt need not have worried about the West's commitment to the status quo in his half of Berlin; it remained firm and constant. But the Western Allies felt no responsibility to the population of the East, whom they had long tacitly abandoned to the Soviets. It was a point that President Kennedy made to presidential aide Walt Rostow early in that fateful August:

Khrushchev is losing East Germany. He cannot let that happen. If East Germany goes, so will Poland and all of Eastern Europe. He will have to do something to stop the flow of refugees – perhaps a wall. And we won't be able to prevent it. I can hold the Alliance together to defend West Berlin but I cannot act to keep East Berlin open.

That prescient phrase 'perhaps a wall' was dropped in without much reflection and not seized upon. As Senator Fulbright's earlier comment showed, the idea that East Germany might seal off the remaining gap in its border had occurred to many perceptive politicians, but it was not an option for which the West was militarily or diplomatically prepared. Nato forces had considered every possible form and degree of blockade that the Soviets might impose on West Berlin and had calculated a precise response to each variant. They had even planned for an attempted coup in West Berlin; the Western forces in the city had trained to combat mobs of communist militiamen who, it was thought, might be infiltrated from the East in civilian clothing and organized to storm key installations under the guise of a 'workers' uprising'. But they had not prepared a contingency plan to counter the definitive division of Berlin.

The final decision to build the Wall was taken at a Warsaw Pact meeting in Moscow on August 3-5. All other possible solutions to the emigration crisis had been rejected. The Western powers could not be forced out of West Berlin; the East German population could not be persuaded or bullied into staying put; police checks on road and rail routes into East Berlin had failed to halt the exodus. The one other option available was to build a barrier around all of Berlin, severing East Berlin from East Germany. This

was physically feasible, legal under the terms of international agreements on Berlin, and would involve no risk of confrontation with the West, as long as access routes to West Germany remained open. But it would be economically crippling for East Berlin and would leave East Germany in the absurd position of denying its citizens access to their own capital city.

All other solutions being rejected, Ulbricht was therefore authorized to put into operation his plan to seal off West Berlin from East Germany. It was to be an exclusively East German operation; Soviet forces would withdraw to a circle around Berlin while the GDR Army, Vopos and Grepos (border police) put up the new barrier. In effect, the Soviet Union was abandoning the four-power agreement on Berlin and handing over its half of the city to East Germany. The East German border would henceforth run through the middle of Berlin.

None of the communist leaders felt any enthusiasm for building the Wall. They were well aware that it offered the West a golden opportunity for propaganda. They were also unsure whether they could carry off the operation successfully. Under the Potsdam agreement, restricting access between the Soviet and Western sectors of Berlin was illegal. The Western forces in the city (5000 American, 4000 British and 2000 French) might intervene to guarantee freedom of movement. The reaction of East German

RIGHT: A British armored vehicle bars the way to the Brandenburg Gate at the boundary of the British sector. In general, Western forces and the West German police tried to prevent demonstrations or assaults on the Wall, and thus made the success of the communist operation more sure.

BELOW: On the western side of the Wall, anguished Berliners climb on stepladders in the hope of catching a glimpse of relatives in the East.

troops and police, many of whom were of uncertain loyalties, could not be absolutely relied upon. Pressured by determined Western troops or angry crowds, they might crack. If there was a fiasco, Soviet troops would have to intervene, even at risk of war. Khrushchev had spent the whole summer reiterating threats of nuclear war and appeals for peace. He calculated that, as long as the minds of American policymakers were sufficiently concentrated on the risks of a nuclear holocaust, they would hold their forces back from intervention in Berlin.

Erich Honecker set in motion the preparations for dividing the city with efficiency and impeccable secrecy;

astonishingly, in a city of spies, no one knew for certain what was afoot. The start of the operation was set for midnight on Saturday, August 12, the middle point of a summer holiday weekend, when both Western political leaders and the population of Berlin would be least prepared and slowest to react. By this time, the panic to flee East Germany had reached its climax. On August 9, a total of 1926 refugees were registered at the West Berlin reception centers in a single day. Many more were being prevented from emigrating only through the efforts of the Vopos, who were turning back or arresting any travelers heading for East Berlin who excited their suspicions. Would-be refugees had taken to getting off their train at a stop well short of Berlin and then finishing the journey to the city across country on foot, avoiding as best they could the attentions of local militiamen. Families split up for the journey to the West, since traveling together they were more likely to be stopped. Spouses and children would meet up again with joy and relief in the Marienfelde reception center – or discover that one or more of their number had not made it through the police net. Coping with the influx of refugees was taxing the West Berlin authorities to the limits. They depended on gifts of US Army rations to keep the emi-

grants adequately fed, until enough chartered aircraft could be found to shift them on to West Germany. There were many people in the West as well as the East who felt this mass migration could not continue indefinitely. But when the blow fell, it caught everyone unprepared.

Just after 1.00 am on the morning of August 13, the East German news agency ADN issued a statement denouncing the 'deceit, bribery and blackmail' employed by the West German government to 'induce certain unstable elements in the German Democratic Republic to leave for West Germany.' This had forced the Warsaw Pact to propose that 'reliable safeguards and effective control be established around the whole territory of West Berlin.' By the time this announcement was rattling off the teleprinters, lines of trucks and armored cars were grinding up to the East Berlin border and disgorging squads of Vopos, Grepos and East German soldiers, with work battalions and other ancillaries, to begin sealing off the last gap in the Iron Curtain.

The total circumference of West Berlin measured 103 miles, but the outer arc, where the Western sectors abutted directly on to East German territory, had already been extensively fenced off. It was the line between the Soviet and Western sectors,

BELOW: Soviet tanks square up for confrontation in front of Checkpoint Charlie during a period of high tension in October 1961.

RIGHT: Signalling across the border became a daily routine for hundreds of distressed Berliners.

OPPOSITE AND BELOW: There were many last-minute escapes as the border was being sealed. In Bernauer Strasse (below) housefronts formed the sector boundary and it was possible to flee to the West by entering the house from the back and climbing out of the front windows. One child (opposite) was let through the barbed wire by an East German border guard on August 14; the guard was arrested for disobeying orders.

from Pankow in the north to Treptow in the south, that was now to be barred. The East Germans set to work first on central crossing points such as the Potsdamerplatz, drilling through cobbles and tarmac to fix concrete posts and stretching barbed wire to form a makeshift but effective fence. They worked well inside the actual sector boundary, ensuring that they did not impinge on the territory of West Berlin and leaving a defensible strip in front of the barbed wire. Armed soldiers and police stood by in case of trouble, but it was only slowly that Berliners came to realize what was happening in the night. A few were woken by the military vehicles and the pneumatic drills; most slept on. Late travelers on the *S-bahn* returning from East Berlin to the West were ejected from their trains at Friedrichstrasse, the last stop before the border; East Berliners with early-morning Sunday jobs in the West were surprised to find the underground stations locked when they arrived to start their usual journey to work. Not until around 10.00 am, when construction of the barbed-wire barrier was already well-advanced, did substantial crowds of Berlin-

ABOVE AND RIGHT: When the East Germans went in to block the escape route through the windows of houses in Bernauer Strasse, many inhabitants jumped from the windows and even threw their children down to be caught by West Berlin firemen in a sheet (right). This child was unhurt, but his mother, jumping next, suffered serious injuries. Afterward, the windows were sealed with barbed wire (above).

OPPOSITE: A new-born baby in West Berlin is held up to be seen by relatives in the East, kept at a distance by the border guards.

ers begin to assemble. On the west side of the Brandenburg Gate they confronted a cordon of East German soldiers and police; at one point stones were thrown, and East German water cannon briefly dowsed the bolder protesters, before West Berlin police intervened to control the situation. On the eastern side of the border, there were a number of arrests and tear-gas was used to disperse a stubborn crowd.

It was still possible for those who knew Berlin well, and were prepared to search around, to find a way across to the West on August 13. There were many patches of waste ground outside the center that remained unfenced throughout the day; there were ill-guarded stretches of fencing where people slipped through the barbed wire; a few brave spirits swam the Teltow Canal where it formed the border between East and West, including a couple with a young child which was carried across strapped to its father's back. In total, about 800 people

crossed on the day, most of them Berliners, many on impulse seizing the last chance of flight. Of the thousands of East Germans who had come to East Berlin that weekend intending to cross to the West, very few achieved their objective. Lacking local knowledge, and too disoriented by the unexpected turn of events to show the necessary initiative, they milled around hopelessly in Alexanderplatz and outside the Friedrichstrasse station.

Even as the work of dividing the city progressed, it was far from clear to everyone what the East German authorities intended.

The fence might have been a temporary measure, or the intention could have been to exert greater control over travel to West Berlin but not to halt it entirely. The East German radio spoke only of 'measures' being taken to stop the capitalist 'slave traders and kidnappers' stealing the country's population. Many who could have fled on the first day, who were to find themselves cut off from family and friends, hesitated and were lost.

Hesitancy was also the keynote of the Western response. Mayor Willy Brandt, who was in West Germany campaigning as

RIGHT: A 77-year-old woman balanced for a quarter of an hour on her windowsill in Bernauer Strasse, hesitating to jump down into the sheet. Finally East German officials broke into her room and tried to pull her back inside; after a tug-of-war, she fell into the sheet and safety.

FAR LEFT: A newly married couple in West Berlin wave across the Wall to the guests who could not come to their wedding ten days after the closing of the border.

LEFT: A man attempts to see over the Wall using a mirror. At this early stage the Wall was still a fairly makeshift barrier, and the East Germans depended heavily on the vigilance of their border guards to prevent people crossing.

Social Democrat candidate for the Chancellorship, flew back to Berlin in the early morning of the 13th to confront the crisis, but he could not rouse the Western military commanders in the city to make even a show of action. They were bracing themselves for a Soviet blockade and had no plans to confront building works by the East Germans. Only fresh orders from the highest level could authorize them to intervene. But all the Western presidents and prime ministers were away from their centers of power, relaxing at summer residences. Their subordinates hesitated to disturb them over a communist action the import of which was unclear. Kennedy was not informed of what was happening in Berlin until an astonishing 16 hours after the start of the East German operation. After this belated briefing, the President's response was pitched on a deliberately low-key note, promising only that 'violations of existing agreements will be the subject of vigorous protest through appropriate channels'.

Kennedy had spent the summer in fear of nuclear holocaust; his instinct was to avoid confrontation over Berlin if at all possible; as long as West Berlin was not touched, the Americans would do nothing. In private, Kennedy tempered his public criticism of the Wall with the comment that it was 'a hell of a lot better than a war'. The general response in Washington, once the situation clarified, was one of relief. A solution of sorts had been found to a dangerous, apparently insoluble problem; the inhabitants of Berlin would have to pay the price of maintaining

world peace. Robert Kennedy was soon suggesting to his brother how the situation could best be exploited for anti-Soviet propaganda.

By the evening of Monday, August 14, the East Germans and the Soviets could be almost certain that their gamble had succeeded. The Western forces in Berlin would not intervene; the United States would not make freedom of circulation in the city an issue of war and peace; only a handful of East German policemen or soldiers would desert to the West; East Berliners would not rebel, nor be encouraged to do so by the West; and the West Berlin police would cooperate in preventing West Berliners from assaulting the new border. After two days' work the barbed-wire barricade was virtually complete. Only thirteen official crossing points (soon to be reduced to seven) were left open between the two halves of the city, still admitting West Berliners into the East, but no Easterners to the West. The fence was heavily patrolled along its length by armed guards. Less than 200 refugees got across on the second day of the Wall, and the loopholes were closing fast. East Germany's emigration problem was solved.

The desolate groups of citizens who gathered on opposite sides of the fence during the day – waving to family or friends over the divide, holding up babies to be glimpsed at a distance, or simply staring hopelessly across – were learning what it meant to be caught at the center of the Cold War. Berlin would have almost three decades to digest that bitter lesson.

3
WALL
OF DEATH

LEFT: In protest against the Wall, 18-year-old Karl Wolfgang Holzapfel conducts a three-day fast alongside the funeral wreaths commemorating the death of Peter Fechter, shot on the Wall in August 1962.

On August 17 1961, four days after the sealing of the East-West border, the East Germans began to build a Wall. The barbed wire fence with which they had encircled West Berlin on August 13-14 was not intended as a permanent barrier; it was too easy to cross, with the aid of wirecutters, and needed too many police and border guards to man. Gradually it was replaced by the Wall, which would eventually stretch along almost two-thirds of the circumference of West Berlin. For the other one-third, in the semi-rural outer suburbs, wire was considered adequate.

Initially the Wall was an unimpressive structure of cinderblocks, eight feet tall, topped by strands of barbed wire. It was a flimsy enough construction for a reinforced heavy vehicle to be driven straight through, and by no means unscalable by a fit individual with sufficient nerve. To stop people escaping in the early years, the East Germans still depended more on their force of border guards than on the Wall as a physical obstacle. They demolished buildings and cut down trees near the Wall to remove cover for would-be escapers, creating the free-fire zone of the 'death strip'; any individual advancing within a hundred meters of the Wall was officially entitled to one warning shot – the next would be aimed to kill. But in the early years a brave fugitive could rush the Wall from a side street on the eastern side under cover of darkness and try to scale it, with a reasonable chance of success if he evaded the searchlights and the armed guards, on patrol or peering out from their wooden watchtowers.

In 1963 a few key stretches of the Wall were rebuilt in concrete. Then, in the second half of the 1960s, the East Germans embarked on an extensive reconstruction that transformed the Wall into an almost impassable obstacle. The new structure was twice as high as the original Wall, made of horizontal concrete slabs bolted together with wire rods. On top a pipe was laid, denying climbers a hold on its smooth rounded surface. A hundred meters behind the new Wall, the East Germans erected an electrified fence, enclosing the 'death strip'. Inside the strip, brilliantly lit all night by mercury lamps, guard dogs loped up and down attached by long leashes to an over-

BELOW: Two days after the closing of the border, on August 15 1961, an East German soldier flees to the West, throwing away his rifle as he sprints for the border fence. He was the first of many soldiers and border guards to seize an opportunity to cross the Wall.

head wire. The border guards were re-housed in flat-topped concrete watchtowers and concrete bunkers. An anti-tank ditch ran along the length of the strip, presumably to prevent East German soldiers driving across to the West in army vehicles. To deal with any escaper who evaded the guards, there were automatic anti-personnel weapons, including mines and tripwire-operated guns. No expense or labor was spared in repairing and updating the Wall, until it reached its final form in the 1980s as a bland continuum of smooth cement panels, an ideal canvas for spraygun grafitti.

This 'improvement' of the barrier between East and West, its evolution and refinement, began in the earliest days of the division of Berlin. At first the Teltow Canal was an illegal crossing point available to good swimmers but then swimmers began to be shot at by border guards; the first recorded death of an escaper occurred at the canal on August 24 1961, when 24-year-old Günter Litfin reached the western bank riddled with bullets and died of his wounds. Soon barriers were lowered into the water and patrol boats cruised back and forth;

LEFT AND BELOW: The body of Günter Litfin, shot by East German guards while attempting to swim from East Berlin to the West, is fished out of a Berlin canal. Litfin was the first escaper killed fleeing to West Berlin.

RIGHT: Vopos, officers of the GDR's People's Police, man loudspeakers in a window of the House of Ministeries, overlooking the Wall from the East German side. The House of Ministeries was formerly Goering's Air Ministry building.

canal crossings became rare. In some places in Berlin, such as Bernauerstrasse, the border between East and West ran along the street; there was no room for a Wall or even a practicable barbed-wire fence. If the inhabitants stepped out of their front doors, they passed from the communist East to the capitalist West. First the East Germans nailed the doors shut, but it was still possible to escape to the West by jumping out of the windows. The West Berlin fire brigade was available on call with jumping-sheets to catch people throwing themselves from windows as high as the fifth floor. There were some terrible injuries and several deaths, but still people jumped. So the guards went in and stretched barbed wire over the windows. Finally, the occupants were driven out and cinder blocks filled the window embrasures; the housefronts became the Wall.

The furious efforts of East Germans to flee to the West, as the last gaps in the border disappeared through the second half of August 1961, were witnessed and photographed by the assembled world press, which had flocked into Berlin to report the crisis. This poignant and dramatic spectacle made the low-key official response from Western political leaders look inadequate and inappropriate. On August 16, addressing a crowd of a quarter of a million West Berliners, Willy Brandt denounced American inaction and demanded more commitment from Washington. Brandt did

not have the full support of the Federal Republic for his stance, largely because he was standing against Adenauer in the forthcoming elections for the chancellorship (Adenauer's main concern about the Wall seemed to be that it put his political opponent in the limelight; in one speech, he went so far as to claim that the communists had built the Wall just to help Brandt get

RIGHT: By October 1961 most of the windows in the buildings along Bernauer Strasse, from which fleeing East Germans had leapt to the West the previous August, had been bricked up by the East German authorities. The housefronts became the Wall.

elected!). But fear of the adverse effect of inaction on West German opinion did push the United States to make some belated gestures.

The greatest living American, in the view of most West Berliners, was General Lucius Clay, hero of the 1948 blockade – he had a Berlin street, Clayallee, named for him. Kennedy played Clay as his trump card, first dispatching him to Berlin with Vice-President Lyndon Johnson for a morale-boosting visit on August 20, and then sending him back in mid-September as the President's personal representative in the city. Clay's swashbuckling style, which had often been considered excessive even in the heady confrontational days of the late 1940s, was way out of step with the cautious US policy of 1961. His presence in Berlin led to dramas that the politicians found both embarrassing and dangerous.

Allied civilian and military personnel still had right of access to East Berlin through the vehicle crossing at Checkpoint Charlie and through Friedrichstrasse station. To have blocked their freedom of movement, in breach of the four-power agreement, would have risked a confrontation that the Soviets were eager to avoid. Military personnel in uniform and civilians in clearly marked official cars were usually waved through Checkpoint Charlie without interference. On October 22, however, the senior civilian official at the American Berlin Mission, Alan Lightener, was asked to show identification

when driving through the checkpoint for an evening at the theater in East Berlin. He refused to comply, upon which the East German border police refused to let him through. He eventually made his journey into East Berlin and back escorted by a squad of armed US soldiers.

Clay seized upon this incident as a pretext for a showdown with the communists.

ABOVE: General Lucius D Clay, one of the heroes of the Berlin airlift, was sent back to the city in September 1961 to boost morale. His flamboyant and fiery approach to East-West relations embarrassed his political masters in Washington.

LEFT: By 1964 the East Germans had created elaborate crossing-points in the Wall, such as this one at Heinrich-Heine Strasse. The placard calls on all people who wish to avoid a Third World War to support agreement between socialists and communists.

On October 25, in front of a mob of press-men, two military policemen in civilian dress advanced to cross into East Berlin at Checkpoint Charlie. Turned back by the Vopos when they refused to show their passports, they were then escorted through the checkpoint by three US army jeeps manned by armed soldiers in full battle kit. This piece of theater was repeated time and again through the next three days. To back up the show of force, Clay parked a squadron of tanks around the American side of the checkpoint. On October 27, the Soviets advanced their own tanks up to the other side of the border, to face the American armor at a distance of little more than a hundred yards. Clay had turned a border technicality into a virtual *casus belli*, but it was absurd to think that the Kennedy administration would authorize a shooting war over the right of officials to go to the opera in East Berlin without a passport. The following day the tanks were withdrawn on both sides, and Washington instructed civilian personnel to stay out of East Berlin until further notice, thus quietly shelving the passport question. Clay was reined in and eventually brought back home.

There were other difficult moments over the following six months, especially when Soviet harassment of civilian flights on the air corridors into Berlin put passengers' lives seriously at risk. But by the end of 1962 the crisis was over. The Soviet Union tacitly accepted that West Berlin would remain a capitalist outpost in communist Eastern Europe; and the Western powers accepted the Wall as an irreversible fact of life. World leaders came to Berlin to see it, making what they could of it for the purposes of propaganda. Khrushchev visited the east side and declared the Wall 'a great and heroic socialist achievement' – although, in private, he considered it ugly and regrettable. Robert Kennedy visited West Berlin and assured its inhabitants that an attack on them would be interpreted as 'an attack on Chicago, New York, Paris, London'. And in June 1963 John F Kennedy came to make his famous speech from the balcony of the Schöneberg Rathaus:

There are many people in the world who really don't understand, or say they don't, what is the great issue between the free world and the communist world. Let them come to Berlin. There are some who say that communism is the wave of the future. Let them come to Berlin. And there are some who say in Europe and elsewhere we can work with the communists. Let them come to Berlin. And there are even a few who say it is true that communism is an evil system, but it permits us to make economic progress. *Lasst sie nach Berlin kommen.* Let them come to Berlin . . . All free men, wherever they may live, are citizens of Berlin, and, therefore, as a free man, I take pride in the words '*Ich bin ein Berliner.*'

This was stirring rhetoric and Kennedy received a hero's welcome from the local population. But after the tepid American

RIGHT: An American tank at Checkpoint Charlie, surrounded by curious onlookers, during the confrontation of October 27 1961. By ordering armored vehicles to the border, General Clay turned a dispute over a procedural technicality into a direct confrontation between the US and Soviet armed forces.

response to the building of the Wall, there was always an edge of cynicism in West Berlin's attitude toward the United States. This cynicism may explain why Berlin wits took such delight in spreading the malicious joke that Kennedy had called himself a jam-filled doughnut – known as a '*Berliner*' in German cakeshops. It certainly explains a change in Willy Brandt's approach to German reunification. Brandt realized that the United States was only paying lip-service to reunification and was, in reality, quite content to accept the permanent division of Germany between East and West. He saw that the only path forward would lie in an independent West German policy of negotiation and rapprochement with the East; this was the policy he was to put into effect, first as mayor of West Berlin and then as Federal Chancellor in the early 1970s. Although fully satisfactory to no one, the Wall suited most interested parties to the Berlin dispute well enough. For the Soviets and East Germans it stopped the mass emigration, if at the price of a propaganda defeat. For the Western powers it stabilized a dangerous part of the world, averted the risk of war and provided a propaganda advantage. Even some West Germans welcomed the Wall: there was an argument that continued emigration would have replaced the German population of the East by Slavs or Hungarians, thus permanently shifting the border of the Germanic world even further westward. But for East Germans desperate to escape from intoler-

able lives under a communist system they despised, and for thousands of Berlin citizens on both sides of the divide, the Wall was a nightmare. For them it was not a symbol but a terrible fact. As the months passed and the world tired of Berlin, now become yesterday's stale news, the host of journalists who had camped in the city began to drift away. It was left to the local

ABOVE: '*Ich bin ein Berliner*': President John F Kennedy addresses the people of Berlin from the balcony of the Schöneberg Rathaus, the seat of the city government, on June 26 1963.

LEFT: Kennedy, Willy Brandt and Konrad Adenauer progress through Berlin in a motorcade during the presidential visit. Five months later Kennedy was assassinated in another open-topped motorcade, in Dallas, Texas.

man territory. The Americans successfully asserted their continued access by helicopter and the inhabitants were issued with passes to cross the kilometer of East Germany separating them from West Berlin. Not until 1972, however, was agreement reached on general free passage between the city and this 'exclave'. Steinstucke was not the only anomaly of its kind. At Potsdamerplatz, for instance, there was a small wooded area known as the 'Linne triangle' that belonged to the Soviet sector, although it was on the western side of the Wall, and the Red Army War Memorial was in the British sector near the Brandenburg Gate. Parts of the *U-bahn* system ran under East Berlin on their way from one area of West Berlin to another: the East Germans sealed the stations and the underground trains rattled through these ghost stops, which were guarded in case desperate people tried to use the tunnels for escape. The overground *S-bahn*, owned by the East German state railways, continued to operate in West Berlin, but it was largely boycotted by West Berliners in protest at the Wall and decayed through lack of investment, its antiquated trains with their wooden-slatted seats gathering charm as a period piece in the rapidly modernizing West. The two halves of the city continued to share one another's filth, the East disposing of most of West Berlin's garbage and effluent in return for valuable Western Deutschmarks, while the West gasped in the winter smog created by

ABOVE: A guard dog patrols the 'death strip' behind the Wall, its leash hooked on to a 100-meter-long overhead wire. When the dogs were sold off after the dismantling of the Wall in 1990, they turned out to be much less fierce than had always been supposed.

inhabitants to cope with the Wall as best they could.

The arbitrary line of division across the city, so casually decided in London in 1944, took no account of the simple realities of communications. The village of Steinstucken, home to some 200 families, officially belonged to the American sector but was completely surrounded by East Ger-

RIGHT: In 1963 some sections of the Wall were rebuilt, with flat concrete blocks replacing the original cinder blocks. Over the years the Wall was continually modernized and strengthened.

East Berlin's pollution-rich coal-fired power stations.

After the sealing of the border West Berlin confronted an immediate economic crisis, which was also a crisis of confidence. The building of the Wall cut the West Berlin labor force by 60,000 at a stroke – the number of East Berliners who had been working in the West in August 1961. And about 2000 people a week were leaving West Berlin for West Germany, an exodus potentially as disastrous as the emigration from East Germany that had now been halted. The West German government responded with financial inducements. Berliners were offered a gift of 100 Deutschmarks just for staying put. Personal taxes were cut to 30 percent below the level in the Federal Republic and there were wage bonuses for the city's workers. A huge Federal subsidy, amounting to half the West Berlin city budget, kept municipal finances afloat and maintained the quality of essential services. For young people, West Berlin offered another inducement that was built into its governing statutes: there was no military service for residents of the city, an obligation which weighed irksomely upon the rest of West German youth.

The financial measures taken, and the calming of the crisis atmosphere in Berlin, reduced the outward flow of population. But nothing could restore West Berlin to normality, surrounded by a Wall, isolated from West Germany, an ex-capital city with nothing left to administer, an outpost rather

than a hub of economic activity. Old people stayed on in the city – by 1976 almost 23 percent of the population of West Berlin was over 65, compared with only 13 percent in West Germany – and the unconventional young came there to squat in nineteenth-century tenements, beyond the reach of military service and escaping the stifling blanket of West German conformism and

ABOVE: An armed guard perches on top of the Wall in 1966. In this, its earliest form, the Wall was far from impassable for a fit and determined escaper prepared to risk being fired on.

LEFT: The view across the Wall from West Berlin at Luckauer Strasse in June 1964. The communist propaganda slogan ironically calls on Germans to make 1964 a year of accord and rapprochement.

In December 1963 Mayor Willy Brandt negotiated a deal with the East German authorities that allowed West Berliners with relatives in East Berlin to visit the East on day passes over Christmas and the New Year.

RIGHT: A Berlin newspaper announces the scheme for passes (*Passierscheine*), to be issued from 1pm on December 17, also noting Willy Brandt's statement that this did not imply recognition of the Zone [East Germany].

FAR RIGHT: West Berliners walk into East Berlin.

materialist self-satisfaction. Immigrant workers flowed in to fill the gaps in the labor market: there were some 100,000 Turks in the city by the 1970s. But for the average German, bringing up a family and pursuing a career, West Berlin had few attractions. There was a steady ebb of population out of the encircled city. In 1957 the population of West Berlin had been 2,229,000; two decades later, despite the influx of foreign workers, it had fallen to 1,926,000.

For Berliners both East and West, the most common tragedy after the division of the city was separation from family, friends or lovers. During the first two years of the Wall's existence, the severance of East from West Berlin was total. There were no telephone or postal links between the two halves of the city, and West Berliners were no more able to visit the East than East Berliners were the West. The only communication possible was a distant wave from one of the observation platforms put up on the western side of the Wall for the use of local people, as well as of tourists and visiting dignitaries. As Easterners were kept back 100 yards from the Wall on pain of death, it was impossible to establish any contact. People faced a separation almost as complete as death, and to which no end could be foreseen. No wonder so many Easterners were prepared to risk their lives to rejoin their loved ones on the other side.

Willy Brandt (still mayor of Berlin until 1966, having lost the election for the chancellorship) worked tirelessly to bring some

amelioration of the intolerable situation the Wall had created. Despite his hatred of the communist system he opened negotiations with the GDR, which bore their first fruit in the 'Pass Agreement' of December 1963. West Berliners with relatives in East Berlin were allowed a single visit across the Wall over the Christmas period. Hundreds of thousands queued in the snow to be issued with their passes, the magic sesame that would open the gate to the East, so that they could spend a few hours with their families. Estimates of the number admitted through the Wall that Christmas vary from 730,000 to 1.2 million, between a third and a half of the total population of West Berlin. This heartbreaking spectacle was repeated on six more occasions up to Whitsun 1966, before the East German authorities decided once more to tighten the screws in a search for concessions from the West. There were no more visits by West Berliners into East Berlin until 1971, except when passes were granted to individuals because of 'urgent family business' – usually births, deaths and marriages. The traffic was entirely one way, from West to East, except for senior citizens: East Germans of pensionable age with relatives in the West were allowed one visit a year across the Wall. About one million people took advantage of this concession each year.

Such palliatives were of no use, however, to the thousands of younger East Germans who were desperate to emigrate to the West. In the early years of the Wall, dramas of heroic escape or sudden death were enacted almost daily in Berlin. On most nights, West Berliners who lived near the Wall could hear the alarm claxons and the sound of rifle shots as border guards fired on would-be escapers. Precise figures for casualties on the Wall are hard to establish, but 41 people are reckoned to have lost their lives in the first year, when the desire to escape was most desperate and the temptation simply to rush the Wall was strongest. West Berliners helped when they could. In the early days, for instance, they organized escapes using tall ladders: while someone kept a look-out for East German border guards from an upstairs window in a building on the west of the Wall, a West Berliner hurried out with two ladders, propped one against the Wall, climbed it, cut the barbed wire on top of the Wall, and levered the other ladder down on to the eastern side. East German escapers would then sprint from the shadows of the nearest building and scale the ladder to the West before the border patrols spotted what was happening.

All the variants on 'Wall-running' – taking the Wall by direct assault – were desperately dangerous. The most infamous incident in the 28-year existence of the Wall occurred on August 17 1962 when two

young construction workers from East Berlin attempted to flee to the West in broad daylight. As they scaled the Wall near Checkpoint Charlie, guards opened fire from a building behind them. One man escaped unhurt, but 18-year-old Peter Fechter was

ABOVE: A sentry at the Oberbaumbrücke crossing point helps elderly West Berliners with their bags as they enter East Berlin, Christmas 1963.

LEFT: About a million West Berliners queued in the freezing cold for their passes to visit the East.

The death of 18-year-old Peter Fechter, shot while attempting to escape across the Wall on August 17 1962.

RIGHT: Fechter lies at the foot of the Wall on the eastern side, crying for help.

FAR RIGHT: West Berlin police climb on to the Wall, at risk of their lives, to throw first-aid packs down to the mortally wounded man.

BELOW: Guards finally carry the body away 50 minutes after the shooting.

hit and fell back to the foot of the Wall on the eastern side. For almost an hour he lay bleeding to death, without medical attention, his pathetic cries for help – '*Hilft mir doch*!' – clearly audible. West Berlin policemen climbed on to the Wall to throw him first-aid packs, despite the risk to their own lives, but he was dead by the time the East Germans came to carry him away. Fechter's death happened just four days after the first anniversary of the dividing of the city, an anniversary that had been marked by angry demonstrations on the western side of the Wall. The callous killing sparked off more violent anti-communist riots in West Berlin. A Soviet car, sent into the West to exercise the right of access guaranteed under the Four-Power Agreement, was attacked and forced to request an American military escort. A bus bringing guards to the Soviet War Memorial in the British sector was also assailed, and for a while the Soviets resorted to carrying soldiers to and from the memorial in armored cars.

Despite the high risks, despair fuelled an indomitable will to cross the Wall. Many paid for the attempt with their lives: Dieter Wesa, an East German soldier who tried to escape while on guard duty, shot by his colleagues as he fled for the West on August 23 1962; Paul Schultz, shot dead on Christmas Day 1963; Siegfried Noffke, who dug a tunnel under the Wall to let his wife and child join him in West Berlin, shot by waiting guards as he emerged from under the ground in the East; Marienetta Jiskowski, 18 years old and three months pregnant, shot

LEFT: A hearse carries the body of Paul Schultz, shot crossing the Wall on Christmas Day 1963, back into East Berlin for burial.

eight times. The list could be continued for pages more. Many of these victims of the Wall were recorded by the simple wooden crosses that soon began to appear along the western side, often inscribed only with a name and a date, or not even a name, simply '*Unbekannt*' – 'Unknown'.

The deaths did not deter those desperate to reach the West. The bravery and in-

genuity of the many escape bids, especially in the early years of the Wall, have become legendary. Hijacking was one of the safer methods, at least the first time each new and unexpected approach was tried. In December 1961 an East German train driver, Harry Deterling, took 24 of his relatives and friends through the border in a commuter train. The following month an East German

LEFT: A memorial cross was erected for Paul Schultz in Kreuzberg at the spot where he made his fatal attempt to escape to the West. By bitter irony, Schultz's death occurred just as West Berliners were being allowed to visit the East for the first time since the building of the Wall.

RIGHT: A notice announces a fast by two West Berlin students against 'Ulbricht's Christmas present' – the shooting of Paul Schultz. The students' anger was also directed against the West Berlin authorities and the press, who they believed failed to respond adequately to the outrages being committed.

BELOW: Along the length of the Wall, simple crosses with a name and a date commemorated those who had died; here Ottfried Reck, killed at Bernauer Strasse in November 1962.

passenger ferry on the River Spree was hijacked and forced to dock in West Berlin, where 14 escapers safely disembarked. Much more dangerous were attempts to batter a way through in a truck or bus. Fourteen heavy vehicles crashed through the Wall or the checkpoints during the first year after the sealing of the border; one successful crossing was made by an East German soldier in an army truck (about 2000 soldiers and guards defected in the first five years). But heavier firepower and the reinforcement of barriers made this straightforward method increasingly difficult to carry off. In one of the later attempts, a bus crammed with refugees was strafed with automatic fire until it crashed to a halt short of the border; the occupants were arrested, many seriously wounded.

An imaginative variant was practised by an Austrian who, as a foreigner, was able to drive into East Berlin on a tourist visa. He hired a sportscar that was low enough to pass under the horizontal barrier that the

East Germans used to hold up traffic at Checkpoint Charlie. In East Berlin he picked up his fiancée and her mother, and drove them back at speed under the barrier. An Argentinian visitor carried off the same trick in the same hire car, before the East Germans installed vertical bars to block the space beneath the horizontal barrier. Others drove out of East Berlin in disguise, exploiting the continued right to freedom of movement throughout the city enjoyed by any soldier in uniform. In one instance an East German girl put together plausible imitations of Soviet officers' caps and greatcoats for three of her male friends, and the East German border police saluted them through to the West, with the girl well hidden from sight. The art of concealment was raised to extraordinary heights in the constant battle of wits with the East Germans. The police searched every trunk as a matter of routine and looked under every car with a mirror, but it was still possible to find space to bring an illegal refugee back to West Berlin by removing some part of a vehicle's interior and turning it into a hiding place. On two occasions, four people escaped inside a cable drum, until the method was revealed to the Stasi by a young girl who had escaped, but whose parents remained behind in East Berlin and were threatened with retribution if she did not return and tell all. Such state blackmail was commonplace.

If you could not manage to go through the Wall, you could go over it or under it. On one occasion a huge crane, which was being employed on construction work in West

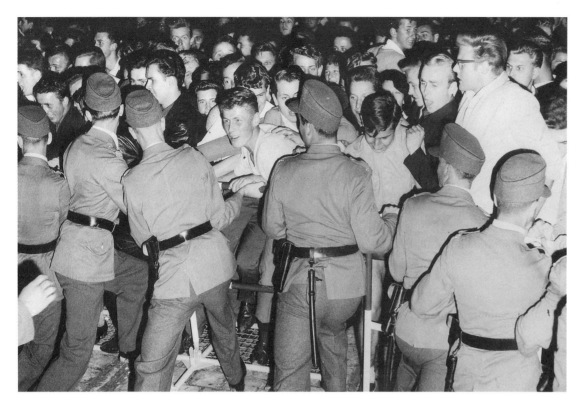

BELOW: Many ingenious methods were employed to smuggle people from East Berlin to the West. This sports car was used twice in successful escapes; it was low enough to be driven at speed under the barrier poles that blocked the vehicle crossing points.

Berlin, was used to reach out across the Wall and lift an East German engineer over into the West in a basket. Perhaps ingenuity was never taken further than in the famous 'chair-lift' escape of 1965: accompanied by his wife and child, a man climbed on to the roof of the House of Ministries building alongside the Wall and, under cover of darkness, threw a weighted rope down to helpers on the other side. They tied a wire cable to the line, which the escaper hauled up on to the roof. Attached at both ends, the cable formed a sort of ski-lift which the family rode down on home-made harnesses.

The Berlin sewers offered a ready-made escape route for those who could fathom this labyrinth, until the East German authorities realized what was happening and blocked the sewers with impassable barriers. Tunnelling was undoubtedly the most successful method for mass escapes, especially in the early years when there were still buildings quite close to the Wall on the eastern side. In October 1964, after six months digging, a tunnel was completed under Bernauerstrasse stretching 160 yards from the outside toilet in the courtyard of a building on the east of the Wall to the cellar of a bakery in the West. Through this claustrophobic hole less than three feet high and 40 feet under the ground, 57 people escaped in the space of two days – 31 women, 23 men and three children – before the tunnel was discovered by the East German police. A young West German who was guarding the eastern entrance shot one

of the Vopos before becoming the last man to crawl successfully down the tunnel back to the West.

The most successful tunnel, in numerical terms, was one which had its entrance under a tombstone in an East Berlin cemetery. About 150 people fled by this route before an abandoned baby carriage, left in the cemetery by a mother escaping with her child, awakened the suspicions of the East German police. Tunnels were considered especially suitable for helping women, children and the elderly to the West, because so many other methods required either exceptional physical fitness or ice-cold nerves. But there was a high failure rate: many tunnels collapsed or filled up with water long before they reached the other side. And they were time-consuming and expensive to build; one tunnel was financed by the American television company NBC, in return for exclusive filming rights.

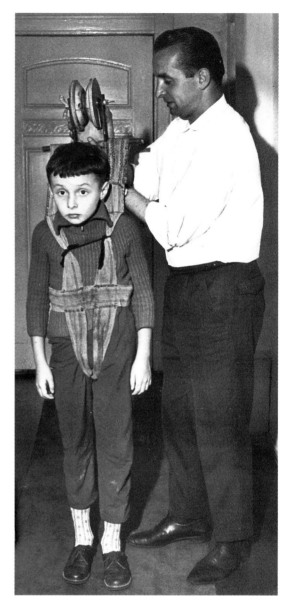

Planning and executing an escape such as the Bernauerstrasse tunnel required skill, dedication and organization. Almost as soon as the Wall was built, 'Scarlet Pimpernel' teams were set up in West Berlin dedicated to defeating the border guards and maintaining the flow of refugees to the West. These groups were quite sizeable – for instance, 36 people were involved in digging the Bernauerstrasse tunnel – and a total of about 1500 individuals are thought to have been devoting much or all of their time to escape networks in the early 1960s. Some of them had themselves escaped across the Wall and wanted to help others to do the same, as was the case with Wolfgang Fuchs, one of the best-known escape organizers, or they had friends and relatives in the East whom they wished to rescue. But most took part simply through a sense of adventure mixed with youthful idealism. The large majority were students, including foreigners who flocked to Berlin like an updated International Brigade, ready if need be to sacrifice their lives for the cause. The foreign students were especially valuable as they could legally enter and leave East Berlin, although they were subject to secret police surveillance and a good number ended up in East German prisons. The East German courts reserved their sternest punishments for those involved in escape networks: whereas simply planning or attempting to flee the country would probably be punished by a 16-month sentence, aiding another person to escape carried a four-year penalty, and operating in an escape organization could bring imprisonment for life.

In the interests of survival, the escape networks developed a high level of professionalism and a profound suspicion of anyone they did not know, including those they were helping to escape. Would-be refugees had to place themselves entirely in the hands of their helpers, who would only provide a bare minimum of information. They would never reveal the date or time of an escape in advance, for instance, since, if given more than a few hours' notice, the refugees would inevitably make some effort to put their affairs in order or contact friends they were about to leave, and thus risk attracting the attention of the secret police. The Stasi, naturally, made every effort to penetrate the networks with their agents and to plant phoney escapees. They were often successful and many escape networks collapsed in a typically Berlinesque tragic fiasco, compounded of deception, betrayal and divided loyalties.

Although officially lauded as heroes in the West, the escape organizations had an ambivalent relationship with the average West Berliner. The majority of the 'Scarlet Pimpernels' were students at the Free University, the university of West Berlin, set up with American backing in 1949 as an alternative to Humboldt University, Berlin's traditional center of learning, which had happened to be in the Soviet sector. Although some of the students were inspired by religious motives, others were subversive non-conformists who had no more respect for authority in the West than in the East. Wolfgang Fuchs, for example, was both an atheist and a Marxist. The students often offended conservative, law-abiding West Berliners through their radical attitudes and their methods; during the 1960s the Wall was attacked on ten occasions with homemade explosives, bomb attacks which foreshadowed the urban terrorism that was to grow out of the same milieu at the end of the decade. Many of the students cordially

ABOVE AND LEFT: The oldest and youngest people to reach the West via the Bernauerstrasse tunnel: a five-year-old child riding up to the surface on a rope, and an elderly man with a serious heart condition crawling through the tunnel blue-lipped and exhausted.

10000 DM (West) Belohnung

Am 29. August 1961 gegen 14.10 Uhr unternahm ein bisher unbekannter Mann durch Überschwimmen des Teltowkanals in Höhe der in Berlin-Lichterfelde gelegenen Wupper-straße den Versuch, als Flüchtling dem Zugriff der Organe der SBZ zu entkommen.

Die Grenze zwischen dem Hoheits-gebiet von Berlin und der Zone ver-läuft durch die Kanalmitte.

Diese Grenze hatte der Flüchtling nach Zeugenaussagen schwimmend bereits erreicht, als er von minde-stens einem Geschoß – abgegeben aus einer Schußwaffe in den Händen eines Grenzpostens der SBZ – tödlich getroffen wurde.

Unter den Schützen auf dem sowjet-zonalen Ufer des Teltowkanals befand sich der nebenstehend ab-gebildete Mann.

Wer kennt die abgebildete Person?

Wer hat den Fluchtvorgang beobachtet?

Für sachdienliche Hinweise, die zur Ermittlung von Personen führen kön-nen, die sich im Zusammenhang mit der Tötung des Flüchtlings strafbar gemacht haben, wird hiermit eine Belohnung von 10 000,– DM (West) ausgelobt.

Die Belohnung ist ausschließlich für Personen aus der Bevölkerung be-stimmt und nicht für Beamte, zu deren Berufspflicht die Verfolgung straf-barer Handlungen gehört. Die Vertei-lung erfolgt unter Ausschluß des Rechtsweges.

Angaben, die auf Wunsch vertraulich behandelt werden, nehmen die Mord-kommission in Berlin, Berlin-Schöne-berg, Gothaer Str. 19, Telefon 710571, Apparat 1668, 1673/74, und jede andere Polizeidienststelle entgegen.

Berlin, den 30. August 1961

Der Polizeipräsident in Berlin

ABOVE: The West Berlin authorities offer a 10,000 Deutschmark reward for information on the border guard who shot a man swimming across a canal to the West in August 1961. The West Germans consistently upheld the view that the killing of escapers was a criminal act.

RIGHT: Two men are arrested at a vehicle checkpoint. As the Wall became more difficult to cross, cars were more frequently used in attempts to smuggle people out of East Berlin, but surveillance of vehicle traffic at the border was strict.

returned the disdain and suspicion with which they were sometimes viewed. Fuchs expressed his contempt for his fellow citizens in an interview with journalists in 1964: 'Heroic Berliners? Hell, they won't get dirty in a tunnel, nor forge a pass, nor help a human being from one side of the city to another.'

Not all the escape organizers were ideal-ists, however – far from it. From the earliest days of the Wall, West Berlin's criminal underworld grasped the financial possibil-ities of the situation. East Germans were desperate to flee and they or their relatives were prepared to pay for the journey to the West; experienced criminals had the requi-site skills in forging documents or passing through police checkpoints. A lucrative trade was soon initiated that lasted through the whole lifespan of the Wall; indeed, by the 1970s, Mafia-style networks had an almost total monopoly of the escape busi-ness. They established a cosy relationship of bribery and corruption with East German officials and border guards, and could usually be relied upon to take a concealed refugee safely across to West Berlin – unless it suited them better to betray the escaper to the East Germans, pocketing the money and staying on good terms with the authori-ties.

The strengthening of the Wall after 1965 fundamentally changed the chances of escape. Once the new border fortifications were in place, with their enclosed 100-yard wide 'death strip', permanent mercury lighting and 15-foot concrete construction,

LEFT: The installation of anti-tank defences was part of the strengthening of the Wall in the mid-1960s. The East Germans claimed they were there to prevent an armored assault from the West, but they may rather have been intended to prevent East German soldiers escaping to the West by driving their army vehicles through the Wall.

BELOW: The Wall in its most developed form, a fortification 100 meters wide patroled by guards and dogs and overlooked by watchtowers, was a formidable obstacle. The smooth round piping on top of the Wall was a simple and effective method of denying climbers a grip to haul themselves up. Wire-mesh fencing replaced concrete outside the center of Berlin.

most escapers had to depend on the use of forged documents or concealment in a vehicle driving into West Berlin. The major advantage of these less spectacular methods of escape was that they did not involve the risk of death. The maximum likely penalty for a would-be escaper, if caught, was a year and a half in prison, after which, in the end, he or she would probably reach the West in any case. This was because the West German government was prepared to buy prisoners off the East Germans, for a fee ranging from around 30,000 Deutschmarks for a manual worker to 200,000 Deutschemarks for a university professor. (In 1964, prisoners were exchanged for oranges, always in short supply in the GDR.) Some 33,000 political prisoners were bought out by the Federal Republic in the period up to 1989. The GDR was desperate enough for hard currency to be satisfied with this deal, which had the added advantage of freeing the country of opponents of the regime and general malcontents. Instead of building up a disruptive internal minority of ex-political prisoners, East Germany exported them to the West at a handsome profit.

The building of the Wall did not put an end to Berlin's role as an espionage center, although it greatly complicated undercover operations in both directions across the divided city. A certain proportion of those killed or arrested crossing the Wall were certainly Western agents, as readers of the novels of Len Deighton or John Le Carré are undoubtedly aware. The city remained a

contact point between East and West, and in the 1960s it was the natural choice as a venue for defections or 'spy-swaps', an exchange of prisoners who had been convicted of espionage offences. The first ever

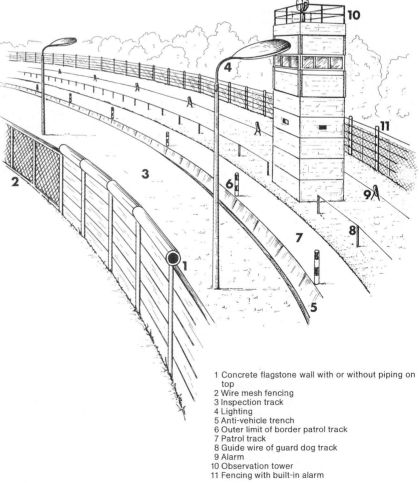

1 Concrete flagstone wall with or without piping on top
2 Wire mesh fencing
3 Inspection track
4 Lighting
5 Anti-vehicle trench
6 Outer limit of border patrol track
7 Patrol track
8 Guide wire of guard dog track
9 Alarm
10 Observation tower
11 Fencing with built-in alarm

spy-swap, which set the model of procedure for all that followed, took place in February 1962. The Americans agreed to exchange Colonel Rudolf Abel, a senior KGB officer who had run a spy ring in the United States, for Gary Powers, the pilot of a U-2 spy plane shot down over the Soviet Union in 1961. Early on a cold, misty winter morning, a US Army sedan drew up at one end of the Glienicke bridge, the gaunt iron structure which linked the American sector of Berlin with East Germany across the frozen Havel. Out stepped Colonel Abel, surrounded by US Army and CIA officers. At 8.30, three Soviet Zil limousines pulled up at the other end of the bridge. Between the two sides stretched the bridge with, at the middle, a white line marking the border. *Newsweek*'s reporter described the swap:

Powers was flanked by guards and wore fur hat and dirty blue pants under his heavy winter coat . . . The sun was just breaking through the mist over the Havel . . . Both groups then walked from their respective ends of the bridge and met at the white line in the middle . . . The two prisoners crossed the border simultaneously. In four crisp steps, Abel stepped over the line and was promptly swallowed up in a group of outsize Soviet civilians swathed in box-cut greatcoats. A US civilian reached across the line, touched Powers on the shoulder. The American seemed nervous but managed a faint grin.

An hour later, Powers had been flown out of Berlin. This tense, unsmiling, businesslike

ABOVE AND RIGHT:The four military powers in Berlin continued to observe the diplomatic niceties in their relations with one another, despite the Wall. In 1966, when a Soviet jet crashed in a lake in the British zone of West Berlin (above), Soviet officers and officials (right) were invited to observe the salvage operation conducted by British military police.

procedure was repeated, with variations, over the following years, from April 1964, when Konon Molody, better known as Gordon Lonsdale, was exchanged for Godfrey Wynne at the Heerstrasse crossing point, up to the ten-prisoner exchange at the Glienicke bridge that brought Jewish dissident Anatoly Shcharansky to the West in February 1986.

As the years passed after the building of the Wall, the panic and drama gradually subsided. All statistics relating to the Wall are suspect, but the change in the level of escapes over the years is clearly shown by all the available figures: a rush in the first 18 months, a steady flow into the second half of the 1960s, and then a decline until it had become a marginal phenomenon. For instance, 41 people were killed attempting to escape to West Berlin in the first year of the Wall; 24 more died over the next nine years; and only 14 in the 18 years that followed. About 3500 people are believed to have escaped through, over or under the Berlin Wall in the first six years after it was built, but from then onward there was a mere trickle of escapees. In 1985 only six people illegally crossed the Wall, out of a total of 160 who fled across all East Germany's borders. Far larger numbers, around 3000 a year in the mid-1980s, escaped via a third country, such as Czechoslovakia or Hungary, and even more left legally after submitting themselves to the lengthy and humiliating bureaucratic procedure required to obtain

an exit visa. As late as 1989 there were still dramatic escape bids – a successful crossing of the Wall by microlite aircraft, a tragically unsuccessful attempt by hot-air balloon. But the time was long past when such incidents had been an almost daily occurrence.

There were a number of causes for the decline in escape bids. One was undoubtedly the increasing difficulty of crossing the border, and another the simple fact that most of those keenest to emigrate had already gone. But there is also little doubt that the impulse to flee the GDR weakened

ABOVE: The wreckage of a US jet trainer shot down by the Soviets over Erfurt, East Germany, in 1964, arrives at Tempelhof airfield.

LEFT: In April 1962 two men smashed their way through the Wall in a reinforced truck at Boyenstrasse. Such incidents forced the East Germans to reconstruct the Wall in more solid materials.

between the mid-1960s and the resurgence of emigration in the 1980s. One contributory factor in the panic of 1961 had been a feeling that, once the border was closed, the East German authorities would be able to 'do what they liked' with the population. The drama of the shootings on the Wall and the tough crackdown which followed August 13, with widespread arrests and an intensification of ideological pressure, seemed to confirm the worst popular fears. But once the immediate crisis subsided, the East German economy began to feel the advantages of using a labor force that was no longer leaking away to the West. Combined with a new emphasis on the production of consumer goods, an economic upturn brought real advantages to the mass of the population. By 1965, almost half the households in East Germany had a television set, compared with only one in 20 at the end of the 1950s; more than a quarter owned refrigerators and washing machines, and the number was increasing rapidly. In 1967, *Newsweek* reported that shop windows in East Berlin were 'crammed with consumer goods'. That same year working hours were cut, with all East Germany's industrial workers granted a statutory five-day week. The country might still be poor and shabby compared with West Germany, but its population was unmistakeably more affluent than ever before.

The omnipresent Stasi network of informers remained a hated and despised infection in the body of society, and there was neither respect nor affection felt for the ruling clique in its securely guarded compound in the Berlin suburb of Pankow. Yet the tawdry rituals of state communism – the mindless formulae of the political sloganeers parroted by the centralized media, the obligatory works' meetings to declare solidarity with the workers of Cuba or Angola – were easily shrugged off. The May Day parade was a good day out for the family, the communist youth organization an acceptable context for harmless outdoor activities and camping holidays. The unpoliticized majority of people were able to live essentially private existences with little interference from the state, which did not pursue them into the innermost recesses of their lives. As John Borneman wrote in his book *After the Wall*: 'The East displayed a consistent colonization of public space . . . while private space was left a free zone for dreaming'. There was always the risk of falling foul of the authorities in some way but everyone knew that, as journalist Gunter Gaus put it, 'The rules are clear, and as long as you stick to them, nothing will happen to you'.

An improving standard of living and a withdrawal into the free space of private life did not reconcile the majority of the East German population to its rulers, but it made resigned acceptance a more comfortable option. With the passing of the years, East Germans became more conscious of their independent identity, a development that was deliberately promoted by the country's propaganda organs, especially through

RIGHT: East German motorized infantry on parade for the 1962 May Day celebrations in East Berlin. The army was central to the GDR's carefully propagated self-image as a disciplined, orderly, united society.

sport. The success of East German athletes in the Tokyo Olympics of 1964, when they performed as part of a combined German team, was a considerable source of local pride. East Germany was then accepted as an independent participant in Olympic events and, thanks to heavy state investment in sports facilities and training, built up a triumphant record in competition after

competition. The sight of East German athletes collecting their gold and silver medals played no small part in promoting a new sense of separate national identity.

Despite the now complete ban on travel to the West, East Germans were well aware of the advantages of life in the capitalist world. As the ownership of television sets became widespread through the 1960s, the

LEFT: The 20th anniversary of the founding of the GDR was celebrated with neon in Alexanderplatz, the heart of East Berlin, in 1969. In the background is the futuristic Teletower (*Fernsehturm*), the most prominent feature of the Berlin skyline.

RIGHT: The 1960s brought a modest prosperity to the people of East Germany, as economic priorities turned from heavy industry to the production of consumer goods. East Berlin was the showcase of the GDR and received the best of such goods as were available.

BELOW: The monumental-style 1950s workers' housing of Karl-Marx Allee, formerly Stalinallee, was preferable to the more anonymous apartment blocks that proliferated in the redevelopment of East Berlin during the 1960s and 1970s. The poor quality of housing was one of the worst aspects of everyday life in the GDR.

citizens of the GDR tuned in to West German TV stations. As one East Berlin resident told an American journalist: 'During the day we live in the GDR; at night, through TV, we escape to the West'. At first the East German authorities tried to block this form of escape as well, but from 1974 onward watching western television was officially tolerated, and in the 1980s the GDR even decided to instal a cable so that the

Dresden area, previously out of range, could join the rest of the country in receiving western programs. East Germans lapped up the advertisements for goods they could not buy and the imported American series that were equally an advertisement for an inaccessibly luxurious lifestyle. But they also switched on in their millions to watch the West German news programs and documentaries. Paradoxically, this gave East Germans a more cynical view of the West than was prevalent in the rest of communist Eastern Europe. They were confronted by the reality of the economic and social problems that plagued the capitalist world and witnessed on their screens the upheaval and disorder that afflicted the West at the time of the Vietnam War, student revolt and urban terrorism.

These phenomena were near to home. West Berlin, with its dense concentration of the rootless and disaffected young, became one of the focal points for the internecine violence that shook the social order across the Western world in the 1960s and 1970s. Left-wing students at the Free University mobilized around causes both parochial and global, from university reform to the Vietnam War and oppression in the Third World, but their chief objective, openly declared or implicit, was to attack the conservative complacency of West German society and show up the liberal democratic order as no more than a front for the covert continuance of Naziism. Berlin was once again the scene of streetfighting, but this time in the West rather than the East.

Although there were instances of New Left radicalism in West Berlin as early as 1964, trouble started in earnest on June 2 1967, when a student called Benno Ohnesorg was shot dead by a police gun during the repression of demonstrations against an official visit by the Shah of Iran. The shock of this outrage stimulated further protest. The presence of American forces made Berlin an obvious target for anti-Vietnam War demonstrations and students convened an International Vietnam Congress in the city in February 1968. The most radical leftists planned to storm the American barracks and call on black GIs to mutiny. Although this did not happen, the demonstration that ended the Congress was, in its time and place, an extraordinary spectacle, as a British participant, Tariq Ali, commented:

Twenty thousand people marching with red flags in what was the capital of the Cold War! Phenomenal, absolutely phenomenal!

BELOW: In the second half of the 1960s, West Berlin became a major center of left-wing student activism, focused on the Free University. In February 1968 an International Vietnam Congress brought students to the city from all over the world to protest against the Vietnam War; they marched through the streets of West Berlin carrying Viet Cong flags and portraits of communist heroes such as Ho Chi Minh and Che Guevara.

RIGHT: West Berlin student leader Rudi Dutschke, photographed during the Vietnam War protests of February 1968. Two months later Dutschke was shot and seriously wounded by a right-wing extremist.

Majority opinion in West Berlin was astonished and outraged at this upsurge of Marxist revolutionary sentiment on their side of the Wall, and a counter-demonstration brought 80,000 people on to the streets. But disturbances continued. When the most prominent student leader, Rudi Dutschke, was shot by a right-wing gunman outside a Berlin pharmacy in April 1968, young protestors ran riot, fighting running battles with police, besieging the headquarters of the right-wing Springer Press publishing empire and setting fire to newspaper trucks. The Free University remained a center of left-wing agitation well into the 1970s; indeed, the street disturbances did not reach their peak until May 1970, when rioters protesting the American invasion of Cambodia rampaged through the center of West Berlin, wrecking automobiles, breaking the windows of banks and American companies, and injuring more than 200 policemen sent in to quell the protests.

The notorious child of the protest movement was the terrorism of the Red Army Fraction (or 'Faction' as it is often erroneously called), led by Andreas Baader and Ulrike Meinhof. Their terror campaign, which cost around 50 lives in the 1970s, goaded the Federal Republic into repressive legislation and heavy-handed policing that awoke uncomfortable memories of the recent past. A law banning ex-members of 'subversive' organizations from civil service jobs, including the teaching profession, struck a severe blow at the large number of university graduates who had briefly joined an extreme left-wing group during the

RIGHT: The attempted assassination of Dutschke triggered off violent demonstrations by left-wing students in West Berlin. Here water cannon are turned on protesters.

phase of youthful radicalism in the late 1960s. It created in the West an embarrassing resemblance to the oppressive system in East Germany, under which a failure to identify with the ruling ideology, whether through political non-conformism or religious belief, would lead to the denial of educational or employment opportunities.

At the very least, the political disturbances of this period blurred the confident distinction between the 'Free World' on one side of the Wall and 'communist totalitarianism' on the other. Being above all else *Germans*, the majority of the inhabitants of the GDR had a deeply rooted distaste for disorder and were not impressed by the spectacle of rioting, terrorism and rising crime in the West. The communist government was not averse to exploiting this traditional feeling for law and discipline. The adoption of the old goosestep by parts of the GDR armed forces may have given Western propagandists a field-day, but it did not necessarily displease conservative East Germans. As Timothy Garton Ash wrote:

The Soviet-model socialism of the GDR sits far more easily ... on the undemocratic, illiberal and militaristic part of the Prusso-German heritage.

East Germans were encouraged to view their society as superior to the West in its order and cleanliness, its honesty and discipline, its provision of health care and education and its concern for traditional culture. To a considerable degree this was a view of themselves East Germans were prepared to accept, and established a counter-weight to the lure of West German opulence, freedom of travel, excitement and breadth of opportunity.

Eventually, as Ken Smith wrote in his book *Berlin: Coming in from the Cold*:

For West Berliners the Wall became a bore, a cliché. The Wall and the enclosure of the city became normality.

Life in West Berlin turned its back on the Wall, focussing on the new neon-lit concrete-and-glass center around Kurfürstendamm and Zoo station. The Wall was left to tourists and the police. For East Berliners, the enclosure that had made the other half of the city as remote and inaccessible as the Moon was less easy to ignore. The government put a brave face on it, organizing celebratory parades for the tenth anniversary of the 'Anti-Fascist Defence Wall' in 1971, but the commemorative stamp they issued for the occasion carried a picture not of the Wall, but of the Brandenburg Gate.

Whatever progress the East German government might make in winning the passive acquiescence or faint approval of its people, the fact of the Wall's existence negated the illusion of stability. The watchtowers and the wire, the mines and dogs and Kalashnikov-toting guards, were a permanent public advertisement of the shameful truth behind the rhetoric of the East German state: the GDR, the Wall proclaimed, could maintain itself in existence only by the continuous exercise of force against its own population. One breach in that dam and the tide of free movement would wash East Germany away.

ABOVE: Willy Brandt gives a television interview beside the Wall in 1986; it was largely through his agency, first as mayor of West Berlin and then as West German Chancellor, that a thaw set in in East/West relations in the 1970s.

4
THE BREAKTHROUGH

LEFT: A torchlit protest on the 40th anniversary of the founding of the GDR.

On March 19 1970 Willy Brandt, Chancellor of West Germany since the previous October, visited the city of Erfurt in East Germany for a historic meeting with the chairman of the GDR council of ministers, Willi Stoph. It was an event charged with symbolic significance, the first small step toward a rapprochement between the two Germanies since the division of the country in the aftermath of World War II. At the time many observers saw Brandt's gesture as an acceptance that a divided Germany was a permanent, rather than temporary, fact of life. When Stoph returned the compliment, visiting Kassel in West Germany, right-wing demonstrators burnt national flags in protest at Brandt's alleged betrayal of the cause of German reunification. But in retrospect these meetings appear as the first small cracks in the rigid structure of the Cold War in Europe which, more fundamentally than the physical structure of the Wall, held the two halves of Germany apart.

Brandt was fortunate that his chance to put into effect his 'Ostpolitik', the pursuit of better relations with the Soviet Union, communist Eastern Europe and East Germany, coincided with a shift in relations between the superpowers. General Secretary Leonid Brezhnev in the Soviet Union and the new President of the United States, Richard M Nixon, were both seeking a measure of détente, based on clearly defined spheres of influence. Visiting Berlin in February 1969, Nixon called for a reduction of international tension, and that same year representatives of the four occupying powers opened fresh

talks on the future of the city in the former Allied Control Council building in the American sector. The Warsaw Pact invasion of Czechoslovakia in 1968, in which the GDR had actively participated, should perhaps logically have been followed by a new freeze in East-West relations. But the United States was prepared tacitly to accept the 'Brezhnev doctrine' that the Soviet Union had the right to prevent change in Eastern Europe, by force if necessary. The invasion certainly confirmed the realities of politics in Eastern Europe, for anyone who might have forgotten the origins and basis of communist rule in the region. Any threat to the communist monopoly of power or to the solidarity of the communist bloc, even from a reformer such as Alexander Dubcek who was himself a dedicated communist, would be met with a crushing display of military might by Moscow. In the last resort, the power of Ulbricht and his colleagues grew out of the barrel of a Soviet tank.

The ageing East German leader had been especially keen on intervention to depose Dubcek because he feared the example of liberal reforms in Czechoslovakia, witnesed by thousands of East Germans on holiday in Prague during 1968, would create demands for similar changes in the GDR. He was equally dedicated to stoking up the pressure on West Berlin: there were no more holiday openings of the Wall in the late 1960s, for example, and visa regulations for visitors to West Berlin crossing East German territory were tightened.

But Ulbricht's hardline policies ran

RIGHT: East Berliners line the streets for a state visit by Soviet leader Leonid Brezhnev in May 1973. The Soviet policy of detente under Brezhnev led to more relaxed relations between East and West Germany, and between the two halves of Berlin.

counter to Moscow's desire for détente and better relations with West Germany, which could be a valuable source of trade and technology for the Soviet Union. The Soviets welcomed Brandt's coalition government of Social Democrats and Free Democrats, which ousted the Christian Democrats from office for the first time in the history of the Federal Republic. Brezhnev leant heavily on the East German leadership to oblige it to respond positively to the new Chancellor's advances. Out of step with changing times, Ulbricht was forced to resign in May 1971. His place as the effective leader of East Germany was taken by Erich Honecker, the man who had masterminded the building of the Wall, but now briefed by the Soviets to take a more conciliatory line on relations with West Germany.

Brandt understood fully that the key to progress in relations with East Germany lay in the Kremlin and recognized the limitations of his own contribution to breaking down the Iron Curtain. The division of Germany could only end with the ending of the Cold War. As Brandt wrote in his memoirs:

German policy after 1945 was . . . in the last analysis a function of the politics of the powers who conquered and occupied Germany. The power confrontation between East and West has since then overshadowed the German situation and divided Europe. We cannot simply undo this division. But we can endeavor to alleviate the results of this division and to contribute energetically to a process that begins to fill up the trenches that separate us in Germany.

The years from 1970 to 1972 brought a flurry of effective negotiations that tended toward the normalization of Germany's position in Europe. In August 1970 Brandt's Secretary of State, Egon Bahr, negotiated a treaty with the Soviet Union that set relations on a friendlier footing than at any time since 1941; the treaty even left the way open for the eventual reunification of Germany 'in free self-determination', although at the time these sounded like empty words. Brandt's government also reached agreement with Poland, recognizing the post-war border along the Oder-Neisse line and thus in effect accepting the massive loss of former German territory in the east, a move that brought howls of protest from the nationalist right and from groups of Silesian exiles. Finally the Basic Treaty of December 1972 between the FRG and the GDR established a formal basis for relations between East and West Germany. It opened the way for the diplomatic recognition of East Germany by the Federal Republic's Western allies, and for the admission of both East and West Germany to the United Nations. The Treaty also provided the context for a dramatic improvement in communication between the two Germanies: to take one statistic as an example, in 1970 700,000 phone calls were made between the Federal Republic and the GDR; in 1981, the figure was 24 million. The two German states were still as separate as ever, but the German people were less divided than before.

For the inhabitants of Berlin, the spirit of détente brought both practical changes and

LEFT: The US and Soviet representatives, Kenneth Rush (left) and Pyotr Abrasimov, at the meeting of the four Occupying Powers in September 1971, when the Quadripartite Agreement on Berlin was signed. The Agreement in effect signaled Soviet acceptance that West Berlin would continue to exist indefinitely as an outpost of capitalism behind the Iron Curtain.

RIGHT: The preparations for a spy-swap at the Glienicke Bridge in the outskirts of Berlin. The city was the obvious site for such delicate exchanges between East and West.

a new atmosphere. On September 3 1971, after two years of negotiations, the four occupying powers produced a Quadripartite Agreement that confirmed the separate status of West Berlin and finally brought an end to a quarter of a century of intermittent threats of blockade and of harassment on access routes to the city. From this date onward, West Berliners could have reasonable confidence that their island of capitalism would survive indefinitely. The Quadripartite Agreement was followed in December by an agreement between the West Berlin Senate and the East German government that, among other matters, restored telephone links between the two halves of the city and guaranteed West Berliners the right of access to East Berlin. The following year the GDR introduced a Citizenship Law which made it possible for any former East German citizen who had fled the country illegally to return without fear of prosecution. So even the millions who had taken the road to the West could

RIGHT: An aerial view from the Brandenburg Gate down Unter den Linden into the center of East Berlin. The monumental heart of old Berlin was in the Mitte district east of the Wall; the communist redevelopment of the area around Alexanderplatz in the 1960s and 1970s created the same soulless effect of impersonal concrete and glass often found in western capitalist developments of the same period.

visit those they had left behind, relatives and friends they might not have seen for 20 years.

Visitors from West Berlin were allowed into the East on one-day visas, which were issued for a 5 Deutschmark fee at the entry checkpoint. As a further way of milking the West of hard currency, visitors were required to change their Western Deutschmarks into East German Marks at a one-to-one exchange rate, although the true worth of the East German currency was only a quarter that of its Western equivalent. Initially this forced exchange was set at the affordable level of 6.5 Deutschmarks, but in 1980 it was suddenly raised to 25 Deutschmarks, making frequent visits to the East prohibitively expensive for less prosperous West Berliners. In the 1970s West Berliners made over three million trips a year across the Wall; after the raising of the exchange requirement, the number of visits fell in 1981 to 1.8 million.

The traffic through the Wall remained almost entirely one-way. Each year about 40,000 East Berliners were granted exit permits to visit the West on 'urgent family business' – although spouses were never allowed to travel together, in case they chose to defect – and East German pension-

ers continued to enjoy the privilege of travel to the West which the workers' state accorded to those whose work was no longer required. For the rest, their only glimpse of West Berlin was likely to be the distant panorama from the rotating café on the top of the *Fernsehturm* in Alexanderplatz, a classic example of communist bloc 'sputnik modernism' that still towers over the city today.

ABOVE: The Brandenburg Gate fenced off, stranded at the hub of the divided city.

BELOW: The Wall snakes across Berlin, separating two different societies

And what did the visitors from West Berlin find, now they were allowed through the Wall? First there was the always shocking encounter with communist bureaucracy at the border: the queues, the spot searches, the guard at the passport desk trained to study a face unsmilingly feature by feature, his blank eyes flicking from ear to nose to mouth. Then there was the strange normality of the streets, visibly the same city as beyond the Wall, yet subtly transformed in a thousand details, wiped clean of neon and advertising, half-emptied of people, the cars shrunk to tiny Trabants and Wartbergs. The people were different too, less hurried, less talkative, even among themselves. As writer Ken Smith observes, visitors 'remarked that they found the East old-fashioned, calmer, quieter, more polite, the way the world used to be'. It was as if the East Germans had remained a repository of old German values, more sober, kind and neighborly. It was in the West that a revolution had happened, a revolution in attitudes, veering toward strident individualism and consumerism.

Some West Berliners could not be bothered to visit the East even when they were allowed to do so. There are many stories of individuals who had been to London, Paris, New York and Tokyo, but had never crossed to the other half of their own city. Hostility between the 'westies' and the 'zonies', as inhabitants of the East were insultingly nicknamed, was not uncommon and was to survive the demolition of the Wall, but those who wished to could now maintain friendships and close family ties in East Berlin, travelling across for a party, a family reunion, a cheap restaurant meal or just a day out. Contact with Westerners could harm an East German's career prospects and was officially forbidden to those considered to be bearers of secret information, for example, anyone working in a scientific institute. With a little caution and discretion, however, most Easterners managed to receive the visitors they wanted and even had goods unobtainable in the East brought over for them in small quantities.

Friedrichstrasse station was the only *U-bahn* and *S-bahn* stop in the East accessible from the West, and it became the prime entry point for West Berliners. Visas were only issued for a day and, like Cinderellas, visitors had to ensure they left East Berlin by the magic hour. As well as being an entry point, Friedrichstrasse station ran a flourishing trade in duty-free goods; alcohol, cigarettes and coffee sold

BELOW: Young Pioneers in East Berlin. Youth organizations were given a high priority by the communist state, not only because they would transmit Marxist-Leninist ideology to a new generation, but also to encourage group activity rather than individualism, and to breed a disciplined, healthy social attitude.

cheap by the communist state to Westerners. And you did not even need a passport or visa; you could buy a *U-bahn* ticket, cross to Friedrichstrasse, pick up your brandy and coffee from the Intershop and head back home. In his excellent study of life in Berlin, *Zoo Station*, the late Ian Walker parodies the response of an ill-informed American tourist to this state of affairs:

What kind of iron curtain was this anyway? Jesus, it was bad enough finding out Berlin was nearer Poland than West Germany. West Berliners do their shopping in East Berlin underground stations?

During the resurrection of East-West confrontation in the first half of the 1980s, both of the leading Cold War warriors, Ronald Reagan and Margaret Thatcher, came to peer over the Wall and shed a tear for freedom. But the realities of the city's life after 1971 were too eccentric to figure comfortably as a symbolic representation of a world torn between communism and capitalism. When British officers often chose a state-owned East Berlin restaurant for their regimental dinners, it was hard to believe in the rhetoric of the 'evil Empire'.

The cohabitation of East and West was managed with a punctilious regard for legal niceties. This was especially apparent in the anachronistic elements of the occupation regime, such as the surreal pantomime enacted around Rudolf Hess, the solitary lodger in Spandau Prison, with his rotating guard from the four occupying powers. The Western military authorities would occasionally assert their legal position with a breathtaking disregard for all that had happened since 1945. The British military commander once rejected West Berliners' complaints about noise from a British Army firing range at Gatow with the somewhat tactless assertion: 'I am the rightful successor of Doenitz, the last chancellor of the Third Reich, and I can do what I like'. But the East Germans could also on occasion show a scrupulous regard for the letter of the law. In 1988 an escaper who attempted to swim to the West across the Spree was picked up by an East German patrol boat just as he reached the west bank; after protests, however, he was handed over to the West, since it was established that he had had one hand on the bank at the moment he was arrested, and was thus technically outside East German jurisdiction.

West Berlin continued to be an odd marginal outpost, a refuge for the thousands of punks, squatters, hippies, and anarchists

BELOW: Soviet troops at Spandau prison, the home of Hitler's deputy Rudolf Hess for the last 40 years of his life. Although Spandau was in the British sector of West Berlin, all four occupying powers guarded the prisoner in rotation, an extraordinary example of the meticulous observance of senseless rules that characterized the largely nominal military occupation of the city.

ABOVE: West Berlin night-life showed the decadent side of capitalism.

BELOW: The western surface of the Wall became the world's longest art gallery.

the West Berlin police, since it was outside their jurisdiction. When the communists finally sold the triangle to the West in 1985 and the police moved in, the punks and squatters escaped over the Wall to the East, revelling in a well-publicized friendly reception from East German border guards.

Legal niceties allowed the western surface of the Wall to be transformed into an open-air art gallery and jotting pad for anyone with a spraygun and a taste for self-expression. The Wall was actually built one meter inside East German territory, so the surface was unprotected by Western police or cleaning departments. From the Reichstag through to Kreuzberg, the white concrete blossomed into a riot of personal messages, bad jokes, political statements, puns and works of art. Many of the graffiti were left by tourists, for the Wall had become the city's major attraction; London had its Tower, Cairo its pyramids, Berlin its Wall.

Needless to say, there were no graffiti on the eastern side of the Wall. Erich Honecker and the rest of the GDR leadership had no intention of allowing the increased contact with West Berlin after 1971 to lead to any significant changes in East German society. Instead, they launched a drive to prevent the 'corruption' of their people by the West.

who flourished in the shadow of the Wall and periodically fought pitched battles with the Berlin police. Like the rabbits that multiplied unmolested in the death strip of the Wall, some of these outsiders found asylum in the gap between East and West. The Linne triangle, on the Western side of the Wall but officially part of the Eastern sector, became a haunt of drug-takers and deviants, who were able to pursue an alternative lifestyle there in total immunity from

LEFT: In 1981 attempts to evict some of the thousands of squatters occupying West Berlin's old tenement buildings led to demonstrations and violent clashes with police. Many of the squatters marched under the black flag of anarchism.

Known as *Abgrenzung* (delimitation), it involved a new ideological emphasis on the irrevocable differences between East and West Germany, rejecting the idea of a common German nationality and abandoning talk of eventual reunification. The communist youth organization, Free German Youth (FDJ), was allotted an important role in preventing young people adopting the 'capitalist' values they might absorb from West

BELOW: Graffiti on the Wall came in all languages, sizes and styles; the spraygun reigned supreme.

ABOVE: Wall artists came from all over the world to work on the perfect canvas presented by communist concrete.

premises. Long oppressed and ostracized, from the late 1970s the Protestant churches achieved the privileged status of untouchables in East Germany. The communist government decided it was simply too dangerous to confront the popular force of religion and allowed anti-state opinion to be expressed in church without the police being sent in. This small area of freedom was to prove of great importance in the organization of opposition to the regime during the 1980s.

The other group allowed to express at least a mild degree of public dissent from the chorus of praise for the achievements of socialist society were the prominent writers and intellectuals. The East German regime took its writers very seriously and expected them to make a 'positive contribution' to 'building socialism'. But even under Ulbricht, novelists such as Stefan Heym and Christa Wolf, poets like Reiner Kunze and Wolf Biermann, or intellectuals such as Rudolf Bahro, managed to produce writings containing implicit criticism of aspects of East German society, although their more biting works were banned in the GDR and only published in West Germany, where they enjoyed critical approval and a wide readership.

When he first assumed the leadership of the GDR in 1971, Erich Honecker declared that there would be 'no taboos in the field of art and literature'. Many books by East German writers previously only available in the West were at last published in East German editions and new works presented a more realistic portrayal of life under socialism. But this liberal phase was shortlived. In 1976 Wolf Biermann, who performed as a singer/songwriter as well as a poet, was exiled to the West after a concert in Hamburg during which, according to the GDR, he was guilty of 'publicly slandering our socialist state.' Biermann was an immensely popular figure in both East and West Germany, and his banning from the GDR became a *cause célèbre*. Twelve leading East German writers, including Wolf and Heym, publicly called for Biermann's return, but this only brought a further wave of repression. Wolf was dismissed from the Socialist Unity party, Bahro received an eight-year prison sentence for alleged espionage, Heym was arrested on a trumped-up currency charge, and Kunze fled to the West after systematic harassment by the Stasi.

Neither these nor other writers and intellectuals who suffered in the cultural crackdown of the late 1970s could be described as opponents of the regime. Bahro was a Marxist and both Wolf and

German television and from rock music. Unlike other East Europeans, young East Berliners had ready access to the latest hits, broadcast by West Berlin radio stations and brought across the border by visiting friends. A western tourist in East Berlin, expecting the grim *frisson* of a stroll behind the Iron Curtain, might have been surprised to witness, as Ian Walker did in 1984, 'two skateboarders . . . showing off on the concrete slopes that buttresed the foot of the Tele-Tower,' with their portable tape recorder 'propped up against a rubbish bin . . . playing "Relax" by Frankie Goes to Hollywood.'

East Berlin had its own punk and hard-rock bands; alternately patronized and persecuted by the authorities, they took refuge when necessary under the wing of religion, performing their ungodly gigs on church

Heym were lifelong communists. Heym told *Newsweek* in 1977:

I believe that socialism is the form of human society that carries the future. And though a lot of things that have happened in socialism were tragic, very stupid and very bloody, I still am of that mind. But I reserve my right to criticize, to have my own opinion and to state that opinion. I don't live in the GDR to keep my mouth shut.

By asserting a rigid ideology and a police state against those who desired a more liberal communism, an open socialist society, Honecker killed the hopes of many potential supporters of the East German state.

Of course, the fate of intellectuals was not of pressing concern to the majority of the East German population. Like the absence of multi-party democracy, it was not top of the list of factors alienating them from the regime. As journalist John Ardagh wrote of the average East German in 1987:

If he were asked what annoys him most, he would probably put first the ban on travel to the West, and he might then add the distortions, omissions and tedious repetitiveness of the State newspapers and media, which he can compare nightly with Western TV. But more likely he would cite in second place the unpredictable shortages in the shops and the difficulties in getting the simplest repairs done. 'If Communism were less plain inefficient, people would accept it much more easily,' said one housewife.

ABOVE: Some of the messages on the Wall were simple and personal: 'Rosi, I'm thinking of you!'

LEFT: East German army personnel inspect the scene at Spandau after five people broke through the Wall to the West in an armored bulldozer.

One thing the East German regime had certainly failed to create, even after 40 years of unopposed power, was a militant society of ideologically motivated workers. Beneath the revolutionary rhetoric which floated like an oilslick on the surface of society, the majority of East Germans showed predominantly the characteristics designated by the derogatory term 'petty bourgeois': an addiction to security at the expense of adventure or excitement, an exaggerated respect for order and authority, and a preoccupation with small material advantages – joining the waiting list to buy a Trabant, obtaining the materials to build a small private house on a plot outside the city. These were the people of whom John Ardagh wrote when he concluded that 'the vast majority have now come to terms with their destiny: they find that life under socialism is perfectly liveable and even has some advantages' – the advantages of full employment, and of heavily subsidized rents, food and transport fares –'though they still bitterly resent the travel ban'.

So the regime could rely on the majority's grumbling, grudging acceptance of the shoddily secure life that conformism would bring. And it could rely on that 10 or 20 percent of the population that actually supported the communist state: self-interested bureaucrats, careerist Party members, secret policemen, as well as socialist believers and idealists. But that was not enough to explain East Germany's mysterious stability, for by the mid-1980s, the absence of liberalization, resistance or

ABOVE AND RIGHT: East Germans celebrate May Day in Berlin in 1986. Although some people expressed their opposition to the regime by staying away from the parades, most tolerated the speeches and clichéd slogans as part of an enjoyable day out with music, food, drink and dancing.

revolt in the GDR was one of the puzzles of European politics. Poland had produced the great uprising of Solidarity; Czechoslovakia, even after the defeat of the 1968 reform movement, had its martyrs of Charter 77; and Hungary was struggling toward economic liberalization. Yet East Germany remained rigid and relatively untroubled behind its Wall.

There were a few gestures of opposition thrown in the face of state power. Timothy Garton-Ash, a British historian who lived for a time in East Berlin, observed how the inhabitants of the battered working-class tenements of Prenzlauer Berg, who had once opposed Hitler, now stood up to the communists by refusing to vote in the one-party elections: 'The remarkable abstention rate in . . . Prenzlauer Berg reflects a long tradition of protest,' Garton-Ash concluded, 'and a certain unbroken working-class pride. "Why should I take part in a farce?" as one building-worker put it.' Small politically-conscious groups of students and

ABOVE: An engineering unit of the East German border guards works at repairing and strengthening the Wall in the summer of 1985. East Germans in all walks of life were notably kind and good-humored in their private relationships of family or friendship, although the ubiquity of the secret police imposed caution and reserve in meetings with strangers.

actions and ideas that they privately abhorred and despised. But instead of building up into an explosive force, their frustration was directed toward the goal of emigration to West Germany. Poles, Hungarians or Czechs were not subject to the same temptation, not because it was more difficult to travel from their countries to the West – it was in fact easy for most Poles or Hungarians to obtain exit visas – but because there was no 'West Poland' or 'West Hungary' waiting to greet them with open arms. If emigration to West Germany was a safety-valve for the GDR, however, it was also to prove, in the end, the most effective form of subversion. As Garton-Ash commented: 'Emigration . . . is the German form of revolution.'

Through most of the 1980s, it was a matter for speculation among experts on both sides of the border whether the East Germans would once more emigrate *en masse* if the Wall were ever to come down. The balance of opinion was that they would probably not. By this time, a large majority of the East Germans who left for the West did so legally; around 11,000 exit visas were granted in an average year. Applying to leave was still a desperate act, since it marked a person as virtually a declared enemy of the state and the object for every form of harassment. It also required almost superhuman persistence and optimism. The bureaucratic obstacle race was a nightmare that could last years and still result in refusal. Yet applications were lodged by tens of thousands of people every year.

As for illegal emigrants, only a few hundred a year found their way across the fortified border between East and West Germany or through the Berlin Wall. A far larger number escaped via one of the GDR's East European neighbors, such as Czechoslovakia or Hungary, to which East Germans were permitted to travel on holiday or business. This was by no means an easy option, but more feasible than the direct route. In an average year in the 1980s, about 3000 people found their way to the West by this more circuitous path.

In 1984 a new method of escape was invented that was to play a prominent part in the eventual fall of the GDR. East Germans took to squatting in West German embassies in Eastern Europe and demanding a passage to the West. There was a blaze of publicity when the niece of Willi Stoph, one of the GDR's most long-established leaders, sought asylum with her family in the West German embassy in Prague. Over the following months other groups of desperate East Germans occupied the embassies in

other young people organized under the aegis of the Protestant churches, identifying themselves with the concerns of the Greens and the peace movement in the West, and demonstrated against nuclear weapons during the height of the crisis over the deployment of Cruise missiles in the early 1980s. Many of these protesters were arrested, others had CND badges ripped off their clothes by police; committed to passive resistance, they constituted no serious threat to the state.

By its nature, like other East European communist states, East Germany created a pool of bitterly discontented citizens; all those blocked from promotion because they did not belong to the Party, sacked from their jobs or denied university education because of their 'politically unreliable' attitudes, forced to express public approval of

LEFT: In January 1985 the East German authorities demolished the Church of the Reconciliation which stood in the 'death strip' on the border at Bernauer Strasse. In general, the communist regime tried to improve its relations with church organizations in the 1970s and 1980s.

BELOW: Members of the East German works' militias march through Berlin on the 25th anniversary of the building of the Wall, August 13 1986. These part-time soldiers were seen as an important prop for the government.

Poland, Romania and Hungary, as well as the American embassy and West German mission in East Berlin. Helmut Kohl's government was unsure how to respond. It could hardly refuse to give asylum to people it claimed as its own German citizens, yet accepting them ran counter to diplomatic protocol and cut across efforts to improve relations with East Germany and increase legal emigration; Honecker had just issued over 20,000 exit visas in return for an advantageous credit agreement with the Bonn

RIGHT: Demonstrators carrying crosses mount a torchlit protest on the 20th anniversary of the building of the Wall in August 1981.

government. Eventually, after more than 100 East Germans had staged a three-month sit-in at the Federal Republic's Prague embassy, West Germany announced that such actions would no longer be tolerated. Instead of snowballing, the rush to emigrate once more subsided.

Internal opposition and emigration would probably never have swelled to sufficient levels to threaten the communist system in East Germany, had it not been for the advent of Mikhail Gorbachev as Soviet leader in 1985. Younger and more vigorous than his Kremlin predecessors, Gorbachev was determined to achieve an economic and political rejuvenation of the communist system through radical reform in domestic and foreign policy. Central to his program was the transformation of the Soviet Union's relationship with the West. Moscow needed to cut arms spending and to procure an influx of capital investment and advanced technology from Europe and the United States. Reversing a 70-year-old tradition of

RIGHT: The ageing leadership of the GDR in the 1980s; Willi Stoph sits on the left, in shadow, alongside Erich Honecker and his wife. They projected a complacent and avuncular image to their people.

paranoia, Gorbachev and his foreign minister Edvard Shevardnadze were prepared to accept the West's good faith, to believe that the Soviet Union was not at risk of attack, and to accept that its forces could be interpreted as a threat by its neighbors. They set out to bury the Cold War and end the division of the Europe into hostile armed blocs that had endured ever since World War II. Here was a Soviet leader talking of economic liberalism, freedom of expression and democracy: not the fake democracy of the 'German Democratic Republic', but genuine elections with opposition candidates and a free vote. Hardliners such as Erich Honecker and Stasi chief Erich Mielke suddenly found themselves out of step. They attempted to ensure that Gorbachev's policies would make no impact on the GDR. Glasnost and perestroika were Russian words that did not translate into Honecker's version of the German tongue. In 1987 Party ideologist Kurt Hager expressed the GDR's response to reform in the Soviet Union in a memorable image: 'You don't need to change the wallpaper in your flat just because your neighbor is redecorating his place'. The East German leadership even banned newly liberalized Soviet magazines and films from distribution in the GDR. But the communist regime in East Germany was the creature of Moscow; if Honecker and his colleagues really supposed that they could sustain an independent existence, let alone assert themselves *against* the Russians, then they had lost touch with reality.

ABOVE: The officially organized mass parades of East German youth with their operatic display of red banners contrast sharply with the personal, somber note of deeply felt protests against the Wall.

LEFT: President Reagan and his wife visited the Wall in 1987, accompanied by the West German Chancellor, Helmut Kohl. Reagan called on Gorbachev to pull down the Wall, an appeal that at the time appeared unlikely to be heeded.

ABOVE: West German Chancellor Helmut Schmidt (left) meets Erich Honecker at Schönefeld airport, East Berlin, in December 1981. Schmidt continued his predecessor Willy Brandt's policy of improved relations with East Germany.

At first no one believed that the Soviets would renounce their overall control of Eastern Europe, even if liberalization was the order of the day. Gorbachev's objective was to establish liberalized pro-Soviet communist regimes throughout the area, enjoying broad popular support. But what if free elections brought defeat for the communists? To general astonishment, the Soviet leadership declared itself prepared to follow the logic of democratization through to its conclusion. In 1989 a Soviet spokesman, Gennady Gerasimov, announced that the 'Brezhnev doctrine' of Soviet intervention in defense of communism had been replaced by the Sinatra doctrine, 'I Did It My Way'. All the states of Eastern Europe were to be allowed to follow their own path – though, as events in East Germany would show, not without a guiding hand from their friends in Moscow.

The failure of the SED leadership to respond to the wave of reform sweeping through the Soviet Union was the final disillusionment for many East Germans. They had lost all hope of economic progress as the rising prosperity of the 1960s and early 1970s had given way to stagnation and inertia in the 1980s. Now the hopes of political liberalization aroused by Gorbachev were denied. Ever since the building of the Wall, despair had fed resignation and acceptance, but by 1989 change was in the air and despair no longer seemed inevitable. Neighboring Poland and Hungary were embarked on the path to democracy, yet Honecker

was still declaring the Wall would stand for another 50 or 100 years. The spirits of the East German people were at once aroused and frustrated.

The May Day festivities in East Berlin in 1989 passed without notable incident: the usual celebration of socialism with parades and speeches, and a cheerful family day out. On the following day, West German television showed the Hungarian authorities removing sections of barbed wire from their border with Austria, one small breach in the Iron Curtain that had split Europe for 40 years. Not even the most inspired prophet could have foretold that this single gesture by liberalizing Hungarian communists would lead, within less than a year and a half, to the reunification of Germany. The most extraordinary feature of the events that were to follow – and they were extraordinary in so many ways – was their breathless pace and unstoppable momentum. East Berlin had had its last May Day under communist rule. The gap in the wire on the Austro-Hungarian border was not an open road to the West. The frontier was still patroled by Hungarian border guards with orders to stop people crossing illegally. But under the guise of taking their summer vacation, East Germans flocked to Hungary in the hope of making it across. Some slipped over the border in remote rural areas; others found border guards ready to turn a blind eye. In the early days, however, over 500 were stopped by the Hungarians and returned to the East German authorities for punishment. The Stasi instigated checks on travellers heading for Hungary, turning back or arresting those they suspected of intending to flee – people carrying their birth certificates, for example, or treasured family momentoes.

Through the summer the new emigration crisis mounted. By August East Germans were crossing into Austria at the rate of 200 a day. The Hungarians had stopped sending would-be escapers back to the GDR, so thousands hunkered down in Budapest, sleeping alongside their Trabants, or extended their stays in Hungarian holiday camps, waiting for an opportunity to reach the West, determined at all costs not to return to East Germany. The West German embassy in Budapest was occupied by a mass of penniless emigrants who refused to be evicted. On August 17 a so-called 'peace picnic', held near the border at Sopron, turned into a mass escape, about 700 East Germans flooding across into Austria while Hungarian guards stood aside.

As in 1961, news of the drive to emigrate triggered off a widespread panic in East

LEFT: The West Berlin police used tear-gas to disperse young demonstrators protesting against President Reagan's visit to the city in 1987. The protesters were demanding the withdrawal of American nuclear weaponry from Europe.

LEFT: The West Berlin police used tear-gas to disperse young demonstrators protesting against President Reagan's visit to the city in 1987. The protesters were demanding the withdrawal of American nuclear weaponry from Europe.

BELOW: The 'old guard' of the East German communist leadership became increasingly out of touch with reality during the 1980s. Erich Mielke (far left), the head of the feared Stasi, was 81 by 1989; Willi Stoph (second from right), the prime minister, was 75. Behind Stoph's right shoulder stands Egon Krenz, the younger man who was eventually to order the opening of the Wall.

Germany. Combined with shortages in the shops and the failure to implement Gorbachev-style reforms, the sight of hundreds of refugees crossing the Austrian border, relayed every night by West German television, completed the demoralization of the East German population. The time for 'making the best of it' was over; no one wanted to be the last to leave. Applications for official permission to emigrate escalated

RIGHT: In January 1989, one of the last official demonstrations in the history of the GDR commemorated the 69th anniversary of the assassination of Rosa Luxembourg and Karl Liebknecht, leaders of the first communist uprising in Germany after World War I.

toward one and a half million. Those who could not wait for official procedures fled, not only to Hungary but to Poland and Czechoslovakia also. The West German embassies in Prague and Warsaw were beseiged by thousands of East Germans desperate to escape. On September 10 the Hungarian authorities announced that they were opening their border to the West; East Germans in Hungary were free to leave 'to a country that is willing to take them.' Over the following two weeks over 20,000 ex-citizens of the

GDR traveled from Hungary across Austria and into the welcoming arms of West Germany.

The East German political leadership was paralyzed in the face of the mounting crisis. In July Honecker fell seriously ill and had to undergo surgery. For weeks he could take no part in decision-making. The SED hid behind empty assertions of the success and durability of socialism and denunciations of the 'traffickers in human beings' who were responsible for seducing East Germans into

RIGHT: On October 5 1989 East Germans who had taken refuge in the West German embassy in Prague were allowed to travel by train across the GDR to Bavaria. For this family, the arrival in West Germany was an end to years of hopelessness and frustration.

LEFT: The thousands of East Germans flooding into West Germany were housed in temporary refugee centers before beginning the hard task of constructing a new life. In the first nine months of 1989, almost a quarter of a million people left East Germany for the West.

flight to the West. Meanwhile Solidarity had won an overwhelming victory in elections in Poland and the Hungarian communist party had changed its name and renounced its past. For Honecker, the writing was on the Wall. Not all East Germans were happy with emigration as a solution to their discontent with the state of their country. In September 1989 open organized opposition to the regime emerged for the first time since 1953, and quickly grew to an impressive scale. The churches provided one focus. They had

harbored peace and human rights groups throughout the 1980s; now a much broader mass of East Germans was inspired to public protest. The Monday night services at the Nikolaikirche in Leipzig became the occasion for a series of weekly demonstrations, growing in size from a few hundred individuals to over 8000 by the end of the month. The Gethsemane Kirche in Prenzlauer Berg was the center for protest in East Berlin. Independently of the churches, the Neues Forum movement was founded in

LEFT: East Berlin's churches, especially the Gethsemane Kirche in Prenzlauer Berg, provided a safe haven for anti-government protesters in the autumn of 1989. They were able to hold meetings and organize demonstrations from this place of refuge.

RIGHT: A torchlit march was organized by the communist youth movement, the FDJ, on October 6 1989 to celebrate the 40th anniversary of the founding of the GDR. The anniversary celebrations, however, turned out to be the beginning of the end for the communist regime.

BELOW: Young East Germans wave their communist youth flags and carry placards declaring the youth movement the 'helper and fighting reserve' of the SED, the ruling party.

Leipzig at the start of September and swiftly established itself as the most articulate political grouping calling for change. Neues Forum was in favor of socialism and against reunification with capitalist West Germany, but it called for freedom and democracy and an end to the police state. This was a position that, at the time, commanded widespread support.

The Neues Forum and church-based activists had a curiously innocent, dated look to Western eyes. With their beards and long hair, their sincerely cherished protest songs, their determination to hold the high moral ground in the tradition of Martin Luther King, they were like nothing that had existed in the West since the Freedom Rides and Aldermaston marches of the early 1960s. The bravery and idealism they displayed in taking on the power of the state, armed only with primitive printing equipment (there were no photocopiers in East Germany) and the frail candleflames that advertised their nighttime vigils, was moving and impressive. But it seemed unlikely they would triumph in a hard world, where powerful outside forces were being brought to bear to determine the future of the GDR.

The first of these forces was the Soviet Union. Gorbachev had decided that

LEFT: During the GDR's 40th anniversary celebrations, opponents of the regime lit candles outside the Gethsemane church in memory of victims of the communist government and in protest at the lack of fundamental freedoms.

BELOW: Protesters hold up a Neues Forum banner on the evening of October 7 1989, opposite the building in which Honecker is hosting a diplomatic reception in honor of the GDR's 40th anniversary. Riot police and Stasi agents later attacked demonstrators and there were violent clashes.

Honecker was finished and must be made to resign. The German communists had to be pressured into introducing a measure of freedom and democracy in line with the new Moscow model. There were prominent German communists prepared to implement new policies and some of these, such as the ex-head of Stasi counter-intelligence

RIGHT: Soviet leader Mikhail Gorbachev (left) is greeted at Schönefeld airport in East Berlin by Erich Honecker on October 6 1989. Gorbachev had been invited to celebrate the 40th anniversary of the communist regime in East Germany, but secretly he was plotting the downfall of Honecker's outdated leadership; the ritual kiss was not repeated at the diplomatic reception.

BELOW AND BELOW RIGHT: Gorbachev stands alongside Honecker during the 40th anniversary parade on Karl-Marx Allee, but the pomp and circumstance cannot disguise the bankruptcy of the East German regime.

Markus Wolf, were already conspiring with the Soviets to engineer a change of leadership in Berlin.

It was a coincidence rich in dramatic irony that the 40th anniversary of the GDR was due to be celebrated on October 7, in the context of mass emigration and mounting protest. Leaders from all over the communist world had been invited to the celebrations, including President Gorbachev. The Soviet leader had become a focus for the hopes of all Germans and his arrival was bound to be welcomed with a popular enthusiasm that would be, at the same time, an expression of frustration and anger directed at the East German regime. The Soviets were well aware of the dynamic of this situation, which favored their own plans.

The other main outside force weighing upon the East German situation was the West German government of Helmut Kohl. Until the crisis erupted in the GDR, Kohl had been a leader with no future, heading for inevitable defeat in the next West German elections and certain to be rejected by his own party in the aftermath. He grasped at the ripening dissolution of East Germany with double eagerness, both as a dedicated advocate of German reunification and a desperate politician in search of popularity. Turning a deaf ear to complaints from some West Germans about the influx of refugees, Kohl did what he could to encourage and dramatize the mass flight from the GDR. Offers of financial investment from West Germany encouraged the Hungarian government to open its border. At the end of September, Kohl's foreign secretary Hans-Dietrich Genscher visited Prague and announced from the balcony of the West German embassy that the thousands of East Germans who had taken refuge there would be moved to West Germany, in special trains laid on by the East German authorities, travelling across the south of the GDR. The East German government presumably made this concession as a propaganda exercise, hoping to improve its profile for the 40th anniversary celebrations. If this was the aim, it misfired hopelessly. As the sealed trains carrying some 17,000 emigrants passed on their well-publicized route through Dresden and Karl-Marx-Stadt, large crowds gathered at the stations. Some people attempted to board the trains and there were serious clashes with police. The communist order was breaking down.

On October 7 the authorities proved they still had the power to carry out their official anniversary parade in East Berlin without interruption: the usual communist ceremonial mix of disciplined military might and kitsch floats praising peace. But when the guests from around the world gathered for the diplomatic reception in the evening, chanting crowds clashed violently with riot

police and Stasi agents across the center of the city. Unarmed demonstrators were beaten both before and after arrest. There were similar scenes in Leipzig and Dresden, where police used even more brutal force.

The protesters' favorite chant was 'Gorbi, Gorbi!' At the heart of the official celebra-

ABOVE: Markus Wolf, one-time head of East German counter-intelligence, emerged as a leading advocate of a liberalized communist system.

On November 4 1989 more than half a million people marched to Alexanderplatz in East Berlin to protest at the slow pace of reform. These banners express the popular view that the communists, having lied in the past, were not now to be trusted just because they were talking the new language of freedom and democracy.

Egon Krenz, a member of the GDR Politburo with no reputation for softness, but ready to carry out the Gorbachev plan to save East Germany by drastic reform. By the time Gorbachev left for the Soviet Union, the arrangements were under way for a palace coup in East Berlin.

The wheels of conspiracy ground slowly, however, while events in the streets accelerated beyond control. On October 9 an estimated 70,000 people gathered at the Leipzig Nikolaikirche for the regular Monday night protests: the number of demonstraters had increased tenfold in a fortnight. Rumors abounded that the East German government had decided to imitate the communist regime in China and carry out a wholesale massacre of unarmed protesters. But there was to be no equivalent to Tiananmen Square in the GDR. Perhaps, as has been alleged, Honecker gave the order for a crackdown in Leipzig on October 9 but was ignored by local officials; or perhaps the tales of blood plasma and bodybags rushed to Leipzig hospitals in preparation for heavy casualties were a myth started by the Stasi, who were busy manufacturing intimidating news items in an effort to frighten off the more timid protesters. Either way the demonstrations continued, and continued to grow. Policing was occasionally brutal, but limited.

On October 18 the plot to oust Honecker came to fruition. Apparently it had been impossible to procure a majority in the Politburo for Modrow, the man who probably stood the best chance of preserving any popular support for the communist regime. Instead Honecker was replaced by Krenz, who had at least the merit of being relatively young, at 52, amid the GDR gerontocracy (as well as the 71-year-old Honecker, the prime minister, Willi Stoph, was aged 75, and state security chief Erich Mielke was 81). Calling for dialogue, Krenz turned his smile on the East German people, only to be caricatured by a Neues Forum artist as the wolf in Red Riding Hood with a big toothy grin. As soon as he was appointed, demonstrators were demanding that he resign.

Over the next three weeks the government made concession after concession to popular demands. Those arrested for demonstrating against the regime were released; there was also an amnesty for citizens imprisoned for *Republiksflucht*. As had happened with Solidarity in Poland, Neues Forum was invited to participate in Round Table meetings with communist representatives and officials to discuss reforms. Neues Forum activists had collected 100,000 signatures demanding free elec-

tions, Gorbachev carefully distanced himself from Honecker, who had risen from his sickbed for the occasion. There was no ritual kiss exchanged between the two leaders on meeting, and their speeches collided head-on. Honecker trundled out the usual complacent platitudes, concluding with the remarkable statement, as his security forces pursued tens of thousands of protesters through the Berlin streets, that 'socialism stands firm on German soil'. Gorbachev emphasized the need for rapid change: 'He who is late will be punished by life itself.' For the East German people, the Soviet leader had a crisper message: 'If you really want democracy then take it.'

Behind the scenes, the Soviet embassy was the center for the planning to unseat Honecker. The Soviets selected Hans Modrow, the Party leader in Dresden, as the best candidate for the role of liberal communist to establish a dialogue with the people. Also in touch with the Soviets was tions. This was the prime reformist demand, along with freedom of travel and the abolition of the Stasi. Krenz talked vaguely about free travel and dialogue, yet failed to formulate a concerted reform program. Anyone with eyes could see that this was not the reform of a regime, but its dissolution. Across the country communist officials were abandoning their posts; some committed suicide. The minor parties that had collaborated with the communists inside the National Front for 40 years, such as the Liberal Democrats and the Christian Democrats, suddenly rediscovered their separate existence and voted against Krenz in the Volkskammer. Newspapers began to carry articles critical of the regime. Mass emigration continued – 200,000 left in the first eight months of 1989 – and serious shortages of labor were developing in key occupations. Demonstrations grew in size and boldness. More than half a million people marched to Alexanderplatz on November 4 and were treated to some memorable speeches by reformers and writers, the novelist Stefan Heym among them. 'It's as if someone's thrown open a window,' Heym told the crowd, 'after years of dullness and fug, platitudes, bureaucratic arbitrariness and blindness.'

Krenz traveled to Moscow at the start of November, smiled for the cameras and stated there was 'no question' of demolishing the Wall. But, probably under orders from the Kremlin, he returned to Berlin ready to swallow the bitter pill of free travel and democratization. There could be no return to repression, so the only road was forward, in the remote hope of winning back popular credibility. In the first week of November Neues Forum was legalized; Willi Stoph resigned as prime minister and was replaced by Hans Modrow; and a new travel law was introduced allowing 30 days' foreign travel a year – but promptly abandoned when it was rejected as inadequate both by demonstrators on the streets and by the newly independent-minded Volkskammer.

Bowing to the logic of events, Krenz decided to institute freedom of travel from November 10. All East Germans would be able to leave the country as and when they wished with a simple exit visa that would be issued on demand. Early on the evening of November 9, one of Krenz's closest colleagues, East Berlin party boss Gunter Schabowski, gave a press conference. He mumbled through a very dull prepared statement, announcing the new exit visa scheme. The full significance of this bureaucratic move might have remained unclear,

had not journalist Daniel Johnson thought to ask: 'What will become of the Wall?' Listening to Schabowski's obscurely phrased, tortuous reply, it dawned on the journalists present that this communist timeserver was, in effect, consigning the Wall to the dustbin of history.

West German television immediately picked up on the story and the key parts of the Schabowski news conference were broadcast and re-broadcast. Did it mean the gates of the Wall were open? It seemed

ABOVE: Writer Stefan Heym addresses the crowd: 'It's as if someone's thrown open a window.'

BELOW: Günter Schabowski casually announces the opening of the Wall.

RIGHT AND BELOW: The celebrations at the Brandenburg Gate on 10 November made such an emotional impact that the change was irreversible.

impossible that such a momentous change could have been announced with such lack of clarity or emotion. East and West Berliners began to wander toward the Wall to satisfy their curiosity, and by 9 pm sizeable crowds had built up at the main crossing points. Puzzled, nervous border police, who had received no new instructions, were confronted by excited East Berliners claiming they had been told on television that

they now had the right to cross to the West. In the confusion a couple slipped across at the Bornholmerstrasse checkpoint at 9.25; the rest had to wait a little longer. The guard at one checkpoint claims to have allowed free passage after phoning his wife, who confirmed that she had heard Schabowski's statement on television; in any case, the instruction soon came down from Krenz to open the border at midnight and let the

RIGHT: On the night of November 9/10, excited East Berliners cross the border at Bornholmer Brücke.

BELOW AND FAR RIGHT: East and West Berliners mingle at Bornholmer Brücke while the first Trabants drive into the West, achieving instant worldwide celebrity.

crowds through. Krenz had intended an orderly, bureaucratized liberalization of travel the following day, with rubber stamps on visas and properly checked documents. What happened instead was a geniune moment of freedom – chaotic, spontaneous, emotional, overwhelming.

As East Berliners surged through the barriers, they were welcomed by an excited crowd of West Berliners and a massive

ABOVE AND CENTER TOP: On the night of November 9/10 young people who had climbed on to the Wall at the Brandenburg Gate began the job of demolition with pickaxes (above). The following day the East German authorities stationed a line of uniformed men between the Wall and the Brandenburg Gate (center top).

street party began that was televised across the world. The dominant emotions were euphoria and surprise; a joyous sense of un-reality. No one knew if the Wall would stay open, or if this would be a single, unre-peatable night of truce in the long stalemate of the Cold War. Either way, the revellers made the most of the moment. Young people began to climbing up on top of the Wall; it was the peak of the experience, a simple demonstration of triumph over the symbol of oppression. There were tears, embraces, drunkenness, a delirium of ex-cited faces, garishly illuminated by popping flashbulbs and the lighting equipment of TV crews from around the world. *Time* maga-zine described how the ecstatic Berliners assaulted the Wall:

BELOW: Everyone wanted to scramble on to the Wall, although the ascent was far from safe.

They tooted trumpets and danced on top. They brought out hammers and chisels and whacked away at the hated symbol of imprisonment, knocking loose chunks of concrete and waving them triumphantly before television cameras.

They spilled out into the streets of West Berlin for a champagne-spraying, horn-honking bash that continued until past dawn and then another dawn. And the daily *BZ* would headline: BERLIN IS BERLIN AGAIN.

Informed of the event while on a state visit to Warsaw, Helmut Kohl flew into West Berlin as the Wall party went on. He had little in common with the mostly young Berliners who were celebrating around Potsdamerplatz. Few of them were Christian Democrat voters, or shared Kohl's conservative nationalism. But the Chancellor knew exactly what he wanted, which very few of the people who celebrated that night did. He intended to claim the night as a demonstration in favor of the reunification of Germany. Until November 9 it had been the radical reformers in East Germany who set the agenda, pressing for a liberal, democratic, socialist GDR. From that point onward, the West German Chancellor took over the driving seat.

ABOVE: After the opening of the Wall, dense traffic jams developed as East Berliners flocked through for a glimpse of the West.

BELOW LEFT: Throughout November the Berlin streets were thronged with sightseers, shoppers and strollers, finding their bearings in an unknown city.

BELOW: The Glienicke Bridge, once famous as the site of spy-swaps, became an ordinary transit point again between West Berlin and East Germany, crowded with ordinary people enjoying an unwonted freedom of movement.

5
LIFE
AFTER THE WALL

LEFT: One Berlin resident views the dismantling of the Wall with a lively interest, but perhaps a measure of trepidation. What does the future hold for the reunited city?

In the first three days after the opening of the Wall, about three million East Germans are reckoned to have visited West Berlin – almost equal to the total population of the city, East and West. The adminstrative chaos of the first night was replaced by bureaucratic order: the Easterners queued for their visas, queued to be processed through the checkpoints – by border guards wearing new smiles like a fresh coat of paint – and then queued in West Berlin to receive the 100 Deutschmarks of 'greeting money' offered as a gift to these poor relatives, whose own currency was almost worthless in the West. But there was still the chaos of sheer numbers: little Trabants and Wartburgs clogging the streets in stinking traffic jams, window-shopping East Berliners blocking the sidewalks, cramming into the sex shops and cheap electrical goods stores.

There was a great fund of goodwill in these early days. West Berliners greeted complete strangers from the East in the street, invited then for a drink or even to dinner. Barmen accepted Ostmarks from East Berliners in payment of bills, although they were worth only a tenth of the West German mark. Easterners were offered free tickets to football matches, free tickets to

concerts. Armed with maps, they navigated their way around this strange city that was theirs and that they had not seen for 28 years. The visitors gawped at West Berlin and the West Berliners gawped at the visitors.

The dazed and happy queues heading back East after the day out carried with them whatever they could afford from the consumer paradise: bananas, oranges, Walkmans, radios, do-it-yourself equipment, dolls and other toys for the children. It was already a defeat for Neues Forum and the liberal communist intellectuals who had wanted to stamp their idealism on a renaissant East Germany. As Ken Smith commented in *Berlin: Coming in from the Cold*:

What the thinkers wanted was a reformed GDR, socialist and democratic, the other Germany, following a 'third way' between capitalism and communism. Meanwhile what the workers wanted, sauntering down the glittering Ku'damm while the lights flashed *Schmuck, Sex, Disco, Mercedes-Benz*, were electronics, oranges, western fruits.

Already on November 10, the authorities set about restoring transport links between East and West Berlin. The *U-bahn* station at Jannowitz Brücke in the East was re-

BELOW: The piecemeal demolition of the Wall by souvenir hunters and enterprising individuals out to sell chunks of the concrete at a profit started well before the official decision was taken to erase the largest monument to German communism.

opened, giving direct access to the West by underground railway. Some cross-city bus services started up and the East Germans began work on opening new crossing points in the Wall. The slabs that blocked the Pots- damerplatz were lifted away on the evening of November 11; the following morning the mayors of the two halves of Berlin, Walter Momper from the West and Erhard Krack, met there and shook hands. The Branden-

ABOVE: Mayors Krack and Momper meet at Potsdamerplatz on November 12.

BELOW AND RIGHT: East Berliners show their new travel visas.

profit, or simply to advance the cause of freedom. Although the police sometimes intervened, the fabric of the Wall was steadily eroded. Yet for all the euphoria, there was still a functioning international border between two very different Germanies.

As the East Berliners trooped home with their loot from the first assault on the shops of the West, a new political battle was joined. On November 10, Kohl publicly made his pitch for reunification. The Chancellor told Berliners: 'We are and will remain one nation.' Many spectators booed. Walter Momper, a Social Democrat leading a coalition city government with the Alternativen, described Kohl as completely out of touch with what was happening in Berlin. In an opinion poll conducted in East Germany two weeks after the opening of the Wall, 83 percent of people said they wanted the GDR to remain an independent socialist state.

Yet the dissolution of that socialist state continued at breathtaking speed, quite unchecked by the euphoria over the lifting of travel restrictions. Almost 14,000 people who crossed to the West in the first five days after the opening of the border decided to stay. As the weeks went by, the draining away of the East German population continued at around 2000 a day. Shortages of

burg Gate, however, now the focus of attention for the world's press, remained closed, declared by Krenz to be of no significance. It was a reminder that the Wall still existed. Individuals attacked the Wall with hammers and chisels, or even with power saws, looking for souvenirs, or to sell pieces off at a

ABOVE: Uniforms and equipment of the East German armed forces for sale in Berlin.

BELOW: Outdated industries and polluted cities were the GDR's legacy to the new united Germany.

lion Ostmarks went west in the first two weeks after the opening of the border for the purchase of western goods or for exchange into western currency. This outflow was potentially disastrous for the already precarious East German economy. Customs controls on the border were tightened in an attempt to crack down on all kinds of black marketeering and sharp dealing that had sprung up instantly as the controled, heavily subsidized economy of the East came into direct contact with the western free market.

The fall of the Wall had been so unexpected that no one had thought through its consequences. The leaders of the reform movement in the East had assumed that open borders and democracy were compatible with separateness. But that meant East Germany would have to compete with the West on equal terms: in wages, industrial products, cultural style. This it could not do. Most East Germans had regarded the Wall as an unnecessary imposition, but it had been essential to preserving a system of government and society. Without it the whole 'socialist experiment', as it was now being called, was destined to collapse.

In the month after the opening of the border, the communist system in East Ger-

specialist skills were chronic and army personnel were drafted in to run some essential services.

The Ostmark was in free fall. In West Berlin 20 Ostmarks were being exchanged for 1 Deutschmark, as against the official rate of 1 to 1. Even at 20 to 1, East Germans were travelling West to change their savings into Deutschmarks, so little confidence was there in the GDR currency. Some 3 bil-

many disintegrated. The purpose of installing Krenz and Modrow in charge of the GDR had been to halt emigration and demonstrations through liberal reforms. But their initial moves were too hesitant, offering only to slim down the Stasi, not abolish it, and talking vaguely of holding free elections in a year or two. Protesters grew bolder and ever more numerous, new political parties were set up, and the old parties in the Volkskammer turned on the government. On December 1 the East German parliament voted to abolish the 'leading role' of the communist party that was written into the constitution. There were attacks on Party property and on Stasi offices. The opposition groups were especially keen to prevent Stasi records being destroyed; they wanted to know the details of the operation of the secret police and who had informed for them.

The newly liberalized East German media were suddenly flooded with revelations about the wealth and corruption of the old leadership. The privileged compound at Wandlitz, the hunting lodges, marble bathrooms, private islands, were exposed to public view. In truth, the standard of living of the East German leaders would not have been a scandal in the West, but it was in

vain that socialists pointed out how infinitely greater were the luxuries enjoyed by the leaders of the capitalist world. The East German elite were condemned not so much for their self-indulgence as for their hypocrisy. As a Neues Forum activist put it: 'They preached drinking water, but in their hunting lodges they drank champagne.'

In any case, some of the shadier financial dealings revealed after the defection of the

ABOVE: A pool inside the compound reserved for the communist leadership at Wandlitz – shocking luxury by the standards of an egalitarian society.

BELOW: The industrial shambles of East Germany.

RIGHT: In March 1990 investigators uncovered a mass grave belonging to a concentration camp run by the Soviets in East Germany during the late 1940s and 1950s.

former state secretary in the GDR Ministry of Economics, Alexander Schalck-Golodkowski, were of a scale and subtlety to impress any Wall Street operator. With tales of Swiss bank accounts and secret arms deals, East Germany now had its own variant on the 'Irangate' theme. A country that had believed its relative poverty at least partially justified by probity and equality of sacrifice was forced to confront the corruption that had flourished under cover of state secrecy. The black propaganda sections of the West German intelligence agencies were undoubtedly hard at work orchestrating this

RIGHT: The site of the mass grave in the Schmachtenhagener Forest, near Sachsenhausen.

campaign of revelations and feeding rumors or juicy titbits of scandal into the media. But the truth was adequate on its own to disgrace the former communist leadership and its regime.

Many sincere Party members who had believed themselves to be working for the good of their country quit in disgust as the revelations poured out. Many others, time-servers who would have joined any ruling organization for the perks and the power, fled the sinking ship. Those who remained in the Party struggled to restore credibility and salvage something from the wreckage. Liberal communist intellectuals such as Stefan Heym and Christa Wolf published an appeal *For Our Country* at the end of November, calling for justice and democracy but warning against the abandonment of socialism and the absorption of the GDR into the Federal Republic. On December 4 Party members forced the resignation of the Politburo and Central Committee, replacing them by a committee of liberal communists including Wolfgang Berghofer, the mayor of Dresden, and Markus Wolf, once feared as the Stasi's counter-intelligence chief (and the model for John Le Carré's Karla), but now a Moscow-backed reformer. A fortnight later, in imitation of the Hungarian communists, the East German SED changed its name, becoming the Partei Demokratische Sozialismus (PDS, Democratic Socialist Party). Under the new leadership of lawyer Gregor Gysi, it hoped to distance itself from the past and make its mark in future democratic elections.

ABOVE: Digging out human remains from the mass grave near Sachsenhausen.

LEFT: Gregor Gysi emerged as an effective leader of the reformed communist party, renamed the Democratic Socialist Party or PDS. It won a respectable 16 percent of the vote in the elections of March 1990.

RIGHT: Erich Honecker's house would seem nothing very special to western eyes, but it was a revelation to the people of East Germany that their leaders, who had preached egalitarian austerity and self-sacrifice, had lived in considerable comfort and had been, in many cases, extremely corrupt.

The identification of the communist party with the state, the essence of Leninism and Stalinism, had come to an end. On December 6 Krenz resigned as head of state, to be replaced by Manfred Gerlach, the leader of the Liberal Democrats. The following day the first round-table talks between government and opposition took place at national level. Soon there was an agreement that free elections would be held the following May, a date later brought forward to March 18. The abolition of the Stasi was announced on December 12, although putting this into effect would take some time. Honecker, Stoph, Mielke and other former leaders were arrested and charged with abusing their powers. An old, sick, broken man, Honecker found asylum in a Soviet military hospital. The communist system had fallen in Hungary and Czechoslovakia, Poland was in the hands of Solidarity, Romania's communist dictator Nicolae Ceausescu was about to be overthrown. East Germany was moving with the tide of history.

RIGHT: The last communist head of state to rule East Germany, Egon Krenz (right), and the man who replaced him in December 1989, Liberal Democrat leader Manfred Gerlach.

LEFT: An East German crowd welcomes Helmut Kohl to Dresden in December 1989 with banners calling for the unification of Germany. German nationalism easily prevailed over the earlier demands for the reform of socialism.

BELOW: Crowds mill around Alexanderplatz in January 1990, as East Germany opens its economy to the sharp winds of the free market. These imported bananas are an exotic fruit rarely glimpsed in the GDR before.

But the German situation was different from the rest of Eastern Europe in two ways. First there was the question of the relationship between East and West Germany; and then there was the linked question of the relationship of the whole of Germany to the victorious powers of World War II, whose mutual suspicion and hostility had initially led to the division of the country and had maintained that division for more than 40 years. The collapse of communism in East Germany implied nothing less than a rethink of the entire postwar settlement in Europe.

In November 1989 West Germany's allies, including George Bush and Margaret Thatcher, declared that the reunification of Germany was not on the agenda. This was partly intended to avoid offending the Soviet Union, Gorbachev was to be encouraged in his liberalizing policies by the reassurance that the West would not try to exploit them to undermine Soviet security. It also showed, however, how well a divided Germany had always suited so many Western interests. Disunited, Germany was a more manageable size, its western half a chastened and cooperative member of Nato and the EEC. United, Germany might dominate Europe economically, develop an independent foreign and military policy, even pursue territorial ambitions in the East. German nationalism had, to put it mildly, a bad record in the twentieth century.

In any case hardly anyone believed that, whatever the popular will, the Soviet Union would allow the reunification of Germany,

RIGHT: Helmut Kohl
acknowledges the
applause of the crowd
during his December
1989 visit to Dresden;
alongside him is the East
German Prime Minister,
Hans Modrow.

RIGHT: Helmut Kohl
acknowledges the
applause of the crowd
during his December
1989 visit to Dresden;
alongside him is the East
German Prime Minister,
Hans Modrow.

except at the price of German neutrality. Perhaps the single most fundamental obsession of Soviet foreign policy for more than half a century had been to prevent a united Germany joining in an alliance with Western Europe and the United States against the Soviet Union. Even the most hostile observers could see that Soviet security was well served by a barricade of friendly or neutral states between it and the West. Everyone in Nato and in Eastern Europe was used to playing by the rules of the Cold War game: internal reforms, even democracy, might just possibly be accepted by Moscow, but any suggestion of leaving the Warsaw Pact or joining Nato would

RIGHT: A row of Trabants
parked alongside the Wall
by their owners, who
have proceeded to the
West on foot. Low on
performance and high on
exhaust output, the
'Trabi' had great kitsch
appeal for sophisticated
Westerners.

surely bring the Soviet tanks on to the streets. The Soviet army was encamped in East Germany in overwhelming force; if Gorbachev ever wished, his soldiers could abruptly end the progress toward freedom and democracy. This is why talk of reunification was rejected by many reformers inside East Germany as gross provocation – the sort of policy the Stasi might encourage to halt the drive to reform.

Kohl refused to accept this logic, pressed on him as much by his Nato allies as by anyone else. He was decided upon reunification and was prepared to use West Germany's economic muscle to move events in that direction. As early as November 8 he offered the East German government economic aid if it would declare free elections. On November 28 he called for a federal solution: a confederation of the two Germanies. Three weeks later he declared his ultimate goal of a united Germany to an adoring and enthusiastic crowd in Dresden.

During December contacts between the government bureaucracies of East and West Germany produced a series of *ad hoc* agreements on cooperation in spheres as diverse as the building of new highways and rail links, the monitoring and control of pollution, laws on private investment, and the renovation of the East German telephone system. They were in essence agreements for the injection of West German capital and expertise into East Germany, to rescue its collapsing industry and decaying infrastructure. Much of the East German economy was placed in the hands of the West German government and of West German industrialists and financiers. Under the guise of economic cooperation, this threatened to reduce the East to a colony of the West.

By mid-December reunification had progressed from being an unmentionable, almost unthinkable, option to becoming the focus of the debate over the future of Germany. Soviet Foreign Minister Shevardnadze had explicitly rejected German reunification at the end of November, but the West German Social Democrats, nervously watching the Kohl bandwagon beginning to roll, endorsed a program for national unity that differed from the Chancellor's mainly in being slower and more hesitant (although they did advocate neutrality rather than membership of Nato for the new Germany).

Opinion polls showed that in mid-December 71 percent of East Germans still opposed unification with the West, but the streets of Leipzig and Dresden now echoed to the chants of 'Deutschland One Fatherland' and protesters unfurled the red, black

and gold flag, symbol of German nationalism. Neo-Nazis from West Germany drove across the border to take part in demonstrations in Leipzig, where they were welcomed by East German right-wing extremists. As the lid of communist repression was lifted off the country, foul emanations from Germany's past oozed out to pollute the social atmosphere. A buried anti-semitism crawled back into the light, twinned, as in Hitler's day, with the hatred of communism; many prominent communists had been Jewish, as was the current leader Gregor Gysi. Communist propaganda had tirelessly reiterated the evils of Naziism, but this had only confirmed part of an alienated, hostile population in its most vicious prejudices.

Brecht had once commented that it was impossible to allow free elections in East Germany because the people would re-elect

BELOW: Berliners demonstrate in January 1990 with a placard reading 'No new Stasi!' They were responding to a suggestion by the East German government that some new form of internal security organization would have to be set up to replace the disbanded secret police.

the Nazis. Applied to 1989, this would be a gross exaggeration: the whole country was in a ferment of exemplary democracy, local action committees coming together nationwide to discuss all the pressing questions involved in rescuing a society that had foundered in economic and political bankruptcy. In particular there was an upsurge of interest in Green issues as people became aware of the adverse impact of East Germany's antiquated industrial plant on the environment. But a large portion of the East German population was unquestionably conservative, narrowly provincial, hostile to outsiders: in terms of western politics, instinctively right-wing.

New Year's Day 1990 was chosen as the occasion for instituting full freedom of travel in both directions between East and West Germany, abolishing visas and currency requirements. Once again there was a memorable party at the Wall, centered on the Brandenburg Gate which had been opened as a crossing point only a week earlier. On the unforgettable evening of November 9, reunification had not been an issue. Now, less than two months later, unity was the theme of the celebrations, its advent inevitable even if its timing was still uncertain.

The Wall remained the world media's favorite focus for dramatizing the great changes sweeping Eastern Europe, a symbolic setting in which a simplified version of those complex political events could be presented with the highest emotional impact. The dissident Soviet cellist Mstislav Rostropovich came to play Bach in front of the Wall where later, in July 1990, The Who would perform their own rather different musical celebration of freedom. Behind the media spectacle, however, all was far from well in Berlin. In the West, the East Berliners had soon ceased to be welcomed with open arms; shabby and short of cash, they had become an irritation and a nuisance. Commuting across the border, they were flooding the cheap end of the labor market, undercutting wages and increasing unemployment. The continuing flow of emigrants was also putting an already overcrowded West Berlin under intense strain; in January 1990 the city council estimated it would need to provide 28,000 new apartments urgently to help cope with the influx.

In the East, the stifling security of the socialist state had been replaced by anxiety and uncertainty. Unemployment was rising rapidly and there were fears that the all-embracing social security net would soon

BELOW: The celebrations at the Brandenburg Gate on New Year's Eve 1989/90 were almost as memorable a street-party as November 9. The following day brought full freedom of travel between East and West Germany, with visas and currency controls abolished.

be withdrawn. People's savings, kept in Ostmarks, were at risk from the uncertain future of the currency. There was the prospect of a general withdrawal of subsidies, leading to rapid rises in rents, and transport and food prices. Workers put in large pay claims and used their new freedom to strike when these were not granted.

There was also political insecurity. It still seemed possible that the old regime would make a comeback. Disbanding the Stasi was proving a slow process; how could the public be sure that the secret 'state within a state' would truly disappear? On January 15 the notorious central headquarters of the Stasi in Normanenstrasse was overrun by protesters and ransacked. The Stasi had directly employed about 115,000 people and another two million informers were on its payroll. How could East Germany be cleansed on such a scale? There were physical attacks on ex-Stasi employees, and they were shunned by fellow workers when redeployed to other jobs. Rumors were rife that leading politicians participating in the new democratic process had spied for the Stasi: rumors that may have been circulated by the Stasi itself to discredit its political opponents. Wolfgang Schnur, the leader of Democratic Awakening, a party allied to the

Christian Democrats, was forced to resign when his past as a Stasi informer was revealed.

Faced with continuing mass emigration – a total of 343,000 people had left in 1989 and the exodus was continuing – and economic collapse, Hans Modrow's government announced in mid-January that it was ready to embrace the free market. Any hope of building a 'third way', a socialist alternative

ABOVE: These cameras were used by the Stasi as part of their vast apparatus of surveillance.

BELOW: In July 1990, Pink Floyd performed their Wall concert in Berlin, televised worldwide.

RIGHT: The Stasi had its headquarters in this huge office building in Normannenstrasse, East Berlin. The organization had around 115,000 employees, as well as several million part-time informers.

BELOW: On January 15 1990, hundreds of demonstrators broke into the Stasi's Normannenstrasse headquarters and ransacked the secret police files.

to Soviet-style communism and Western capitalism, was dead. Modrow could only hope to hold the country together until terms were agreed for a West German takeover of the GDR. Unity for Germany was no longer a political program on which in-

dividuals could agree or disagree; it was the inevitable consequence of a process of disintegration. At the end of January Modrow formed a coalition government with opposition groups to prepare for elections on March 18, brought forward from May

LEFT: The examination of Stasi files was to produce many embarrassing revelations about leading political figures who were compromised as informers. Perhaps as many as one in five of the adult population of East Germany had spied on friends, colleagues and neighbors.

because reunification could not wait. Any delay and East Germany might fall apart in economic chaos.

These were the first free elections in eastern Germany for 58 years – last time the majority had voted for Hitler. Once the campaign started the Western political parties muscled in with their money, equipment and electoral experience, sidelining groups such as Neues Forum, which were simply brushed aside. The Christian Democrats supported the East German version of their party and its allies, while the Social Democrats backed the East German SPD. The result was a triumph for Helmut Kohl, the Christian Democrat Alliance winning 48 percent of the votes to only 21 percent for the Social Democrats. The reformed communists of the PDS drew a surprisingly respectable 16 percent of the total vote,

LEFT: Lothar de Maizière, elected to lead East Germany to unification with the West, addresses the first and last freely elected parliament in the brief history of the East German state.

almost one in six of the electorate, even though a million people had left the party in the previous three months. Christian Democrat leader Lothar de Maizière took over power from Hans Modrow.

Meanwhile the Wall was coming down. At first this task had been left to tourists and to enterprising individuals who had made a major business out of cutting the Wall up into souvenirs. In January the Modrow government, realizing that it owned at least one valuable asset, announced it was setting up a company to market the Wall to museums, companies and private individuals worldwide, estimating the value of its total length at 800 million Deutschmarks. Demolition began piecemeal in February, a simple fence going up to mark the still existing border. The March elections were interpreted as a clear endorsement of Kohl's policies by the East German people, but it was still not clear how close to reunification Germany might be. Two sets of complex negotiations had to take place, one between the governments of East and West Germany

and the other, of far more doubtful outcome, between the two Germanies and the four wartime allies, the United States, Britain, the Soviet Union and France.

The talks between the two Germanies were relatively simple since the Eastern government had barely a card in its hand. The substantial issues were the timing of reunification, and transitional arrangements to soften the impact of rapid change on the East German population. The sticking point was the currency. During the March elections in East Germany the Christian Democrats had promised that, at economic reunification, Ostmarks would be converted into West German Deutschmarks at parity, an exchange rate of one for one, as compared with the official rate of three to one that had been set soon after the opening of the border. This would give East Germans a windfall, in effect tripling the real value of their savings overnight (and in a country with heavily subsidized prices and few goods for sale in the shops, most people's savings were considerable). They would

BELOW: By June 1990 the wholesale demolition of the Wall was under way. The East German state, the owner of the Wall, had set up a company to market fragments of it, which fetched a high price at international auctions.

still be much poorer than West Germans, but not pauperized.

The powerful West German Bundesbank was horrified, however, at the inflationary implications of parity for the Ostmark. It was already accepted that the costs of reunification would be high, requiring a rise in tax levels and government spending, and that consumer demand from the East would tend to push up inflation. A one-to-one exchange rate ran counter to all the Bundes-bank's principles of sound money. But when the suggestion was floated of a two-to-one rate, East German opinion was outraged. Faced with a vociferous revolt among those who had voted for the Christian Democrats in March, Kohl backed down. The date for economic unification between East and West Germany was set for July 1. Most East Germans would be allowed to exchange 4000 Ostmarks into Deutschmarks at parity (in two stages) and

LEFT: The removal of Checkpoint Charlie gave the armed forces of the occupying powers one of their last opportunities for a ceremonial parade in West Berlin.

RIGHT: A delighted East German shows off his fistful of western Deutschmarks on July 1 1990, the day of economic unification between East and West Germany. Most East Germans used their hard currency to buy West German consumer goods, thus worsening the slump in East German industry, which lost its domestic customers.

the rest of their savings at two-to-one. Pensioners could exchange 6000 Ostmarks at parity, and children 2000. In effect, a couple with two children were being offered a bonus of around $5000 on their savings.

As the date for economic union approached, the demolition of the Wall acquired a new urgency. In mid-June a small ceremony attended the dismantling of Checkpoint Charlie; the US guard hut was carried away on the back of a truck. As the Wall disappeared from the center of Berlin, pieces of it were reappearing all over the world: George Bush had a fragment on his desk in the White House; there were persistent rumors that the Disney organization intended to buy a whole section, complete with watchtowers, and reconstruct it in one of their pleasure parks. Graffiti artists who had decorated the Wall complained that their work was being sold to the profit of others; they were promised an appropriate payment. The dogs which had patroled the 'death strip' were also being sold off, although they proved disappointingly tame and many were returned as unsatisfactory by West German security firms.

Economic unification on July 1 was another occasion for a night of beer and fireworks in Berlin. On the stroke of midnight the Deutschebank on Alexanderplatz opened its doors and was stormed by savers wanting to withdraw their fistful of Deutschmarks. Fourteen people were injured in the crush. A small group of communists demonstrated with a placard that read: 'For sale, one country, well situated in the heart of Europe, docile workforce and bargain basement prices.'

Unification meant East Germany being swallowed up by the West, as was plain for all to see. Even the few admirable aspects of the GDR state and society, such as its outstanding training facilities for swimmers and athletes, were to be wound up along with the rest. Everywhere the traces of the communist regime were being eradicated – including place names, with Karl-Marx-Stadt, for example, reverting to its former name of Cheminitz. The tide of revenge swept on: proceedings were started against border guards who had fired on escapers and Honecker was charged with ordering the shoot-to-kill policy on the Wall. Investigation of former Stasi agents and their informers continued apace. Examination of Stasi files also revealed double agents who had spied for the GDR in West Germany, including Klaus Kuron, a senior West German counter-intelligence officer. Markus Wolf, despite his new liberal credentials, fled to the Soviet Union to avoid the arrest that would have followed reunification.

The momentum of the drive to unity within Germany put pressure on the former wartime allies to come to an agreement on the country's future. It was simply impossible for Britain, France or the United States, whatever their private reservations about the process, to resist the democratically expressed will of the German people to unite. The Soviet Union was little better placed to hold up reunification, but was initially determined to stop the new united Ger-

LEFT: An East German
mother confronts the
unprecedented
phenomenon of
conflicting election
posters on the streets of
East Berlin.

many being integrated into Nato. The cru-
cial Soviet objective, however, was to
extract as much financial benefit from the
negotiations as possible. From the Soviet
point of view as well, East Germany was up
for sale.

The 4 + 2 talks, as they were known – the
four wartime allies plus the two Germanies
– opened on March 15. Poland was later
allowed to participate, in recognition of its
concern about Kohl's failure publicly to confirm his acceptance of Poland's borders,
which embraced a large area of pre-war
Germany. The talks were still bogged down
in July when Kohl met Gorbachev in Stav-
ropol; this meeting seems to have broken
the logjam. An offer of German economic
cooperation was traded for diplomatic concessions from the Soviets. Although there
was some tough dealing up to the last

LEFT: Young fascists pose
for the camera during a
Neo-Nazi rally in Dresden
in October 1990. Violence
by extreme right-wing
elements was one of the
most disturbing features
of East German society
after the fall of the
communist regime.

ABOVE: The Western occupation forces say their formal farewell to Berlin at the Charlottenburg Castle on October 2 1990, after 45 years in at least nominal command of the city.

BELOW: Revellers celebrate German reunification on October 3. One carries an East German flag with the hammer-and-compass symbol crossed out, making it the flag of a unified Germany.

price of unity: promises of German finance and technical expertise. But the Soviet Union was falling apart as Germany came together. For Berlin, no irony could have better marked the transformation that one year had brought than the decision to send emergency food aid to the Soviet Union that winter. A vast stockpile of food had been held in West Berlin ever since the 1948 blockade, about 350,000 tons of it, in case the stranglehold was applied again. Now almost all this food was sent to Moscow and Leningrad to help the Soviet population survive the winter.

After the 4+2 talks had ended in agreement, no further obstacle lay in the path of German unity. At midnight on October 3, the black, red and gold flag was raised in Berlin and 45 years of division came to an end. A few hours earlier the Kommandatura, the four-power military government of the city, had been formally dissolved. It was just 327 days since the unforgettable night of the opening of the Wall. Now there was a new German state with a population of 77.4 million. The German President, Richard von Weizsacker, speaking at the refurbished Reichstag building, declared: 'We want to serve peace in a united Europe and the world.' *Time* magazine observed that the celebrations on the Berlin streets were 'nowhere near as exuberant as the crowds that had cheered the demise of the Wall or even West Germany's victory in the World Cup . . .' Perhaps there had been too many street-parties. Or perhaps thoughts were now concentrated more on an uncertain future.

Eastern Germany was experiencing, in the words of *Newsweek*, 'the biggest bankruptcy in history'. Very few, if any, East German firms were able to compete with the products flooding in from the West, or to fulfill new demands for safe and healthy working conditions and limits on environmental pollution. Kohl believed that the answer to the ex-GDR's problems lay in the free market. The theory was that Western capital would pour into the East, buying up derelict industries and transforming them into viable concerns. But in the winter of 1990 this was no more than a hopeful dream.

The complexity of property claims in the East was a social nightmare. Anyone who had been dispossessed by the communist state or by the Nazis had the right to file a claim, whether to a private house or apartment or to a farm or business. Hundreds of thousands of Germans in the East were thus threatened with eviction from their homes, and thousands of businesses were unsaleable because of doubts over rightful owner-

moment, on September 12 the 'Treaty on the Final Settlement with regard to Germany' was signed in the marble halls of the Oktyabr Hotel in Moscow. The Soviet Union conceded almost every point: Germany was to be united, independent, and a member of Nato if it wished. There would be no immediate withdrawal of Soviet forces stationed in East Germany, however; 360,000 Soviet troops would stay to the end of 1994, and the German government would pay 12 billion Deutschmarks toward their eventual resettlement in the Soviet Union. In a speech full of noble sentiments, the Soviet Foreign Minister Edvard Shevardnadze declared that the treaty drew 'the final line beneath World War II and opened a new account in time'. But there was no hiding the weakness of the Soviet Union in allowing a solution to the German problem so opposed to its interests.

In November, a month after reunification, Gorbachev came to Germany to claim the

ship. To this misery was added the uncertainty of unemployment. Three months after reunification about 750,000 Easterners were unemployed and another 1.8 million on short-time working, still attached to a factory or office, waiting to see if it would become operative again under new management. According to some estimates, around 50 percent of the total Eastern workforce might be unemployed by the summer of 1991. For those in work, wages were a third or a half the level of their equivalent in the West, yet prices were being readjusted to Western levels.

The ideological cleansing of the East also took its toll. University professors and teachers were either dismissed, if considered incurably Marxist-Leninist, or sent for re-education. Civil servants were drafted in from the West to take over the bureaucracy and reconstruct it on Western lines. The People's Army was disbanded, only a small part of it scheduled for integration in the Federal armed forces if susceptible to re-training. Everywhere, Easterners found their skills disparaged and their careers set at nought. Of course there were many corrupt bullies and placemen who deserved this treatment; but there were many honest people who did not.

In the face of economic dereliction and demoralization, thousands continued to leave the former East Germany for the former West Germany. Between the opening of the border and reunification, East Germans had emigrated at a maximum of 70,000 a month. After unification the rate was lower, but still enough to cripple chances of economic recovery: in the first three months of a unified Germany, 100,000 Easterners left for the West.

ABOVE: A graffiti artist records the end of the Wall on the Wall itself.

BELOW: The ceremony outside the restored Reichstag building that officially created a new united Germany.

ABOVE: Soviet soldiers on the way home, though some were to stay until 1994.

BELOW: Rioting in Alexanderplatz on the night of reunification.

with the Wall gone, packs of rabid foxes were invading West Berlin. Such stories will always surface when a society's fundamental sense of security is menaced. Other anxieties centered on invasion by Poles, or by ethnic Germans from the Soviet Union and Romania, or by the East Germans.

It was not that Germans, East or West, did not want unification when they got it – on the contrary. In all-German elections in December, Helmut Kohl triumphed precisely because he was the architect of Germany unity. But even politically there were disturbing currents. A football match in Leipzig between Bayern Munich and Lokomotiv Leipzig on September 2 was the occasion for rioting by neo-Nazi skinheads that was only controled when police opened fire on stone- and bottle-throwers. In November there were violent clashes between police and anarchist squatters in East Berlin. Meanwhile women marched in protest at the suggestion that less liberal West German abortion laws should be substituted for the abortion-on-demand that had applied in the GDR, and workers massed to protest the closure of their factories and the loss of their jobs.

In the West, the disappearance of the Wall also brought anxieties. Some of these were practical: fear of inflation, fear of unemployment, resentment at the cost to the taxpayer of revitalizing the East, estimated at a possible £775 billion over ten years. But there was also a vaguer cultural *angst*. In September 1990 there were rumors that,

LEFT: Riot police in action on Alexanderplatz, October 3 1990. East Germany faced a difficult and troubled future as the economic and social strains of reunification took hold.

BELOW: A German cartoonist's Karl Marx comments wrily on the demise of communism in Eastern Europe: 'I'm sorry – it was just an idea.'

In the center of Berlin, Potsdamerplatz once more became a busy thoroughfare and local inhabitants had become accustomed to strolling over the open wasteland where people had once died for attempting to cross. Projects abounded for the redevelopment of the long strip of land where the Wall had stood, but moves to retain a small section of the Wall as a historical memorial aroused little enthusiasm – perhaps because, in retrospect, the significance of the Wall seemed so obscure.

Once the Wall had stood as a simplifying symbol. On one side was freedom and democracy, happiness and abundance; on the other, tyrannous oppression, gloom and scarcity. It was a prison wall and outside it lay liberty, for which desperate men were prepared to risk their lives. But after the Wall was gone, this sharply focused picture blurred and faded. The inhabitants of the East had to realize that there were forces other than state oppression against which people could be powerless to defend themselves, and that the free market and free elections would not by magic bring a Western standard of living in their train.

The events of 1989 made fashionable the phrase 'the End of History'. But the fall of the Wall was as much a beginning as an ending, and the beginning of something quite unknown. As Alexander Herzen wrote in the nineteenth century, 'The future is worse than the ocean – there is nothing there. It will be what men and circumstances make it.' Berlin, Germany and the whole of Europe were launched into a new void of uncertainty, out of which they would construct an as yet unimaginable future.

INDEX

ACKNOWLEDGMENTS

Beier: page 157 (below)

Bison Picture Library: pages 16, 17 (below)

Pierre Boom: pages 117 (below), 127 (above), 131 (below right)

Jockel Finck/Zenit: pages 120 (above), 122 (below)

Dietmar Gust/Zenit: pages 121 (above), 153 (below)

Bernd Heinz: pages 118 (above), 140 (below), 141 (above)

Imperial War Museum: page 18 (below)

Landesbildstelle, Berlin: pages 8, 9 (below), 14, 15 (both), 19 (both), 20, 25, (above), 27 (both), 28, 32, 33, 35 (both), 36 (above), 37 (both), 39 (both), 40, 42, 43 (both), 44, 45 (both), 46, 47 (both), 48 (both), 49 (both), 50 (both), 51, 52, 53, 54 (both), 55, 56, 57 (below), 58, 59, 61 (both), 62 (both), 63, 64 (below), 66 (left), 69 (both), 70, 72, 73 (below), 74 (both), 75 (both), 76, 77 (both), 78 (below), 79 (below), 80 (both), 81 (both), 82 (below), 83 (both), 84 (both), 86 (below), 89 (above), 90 (both), 91 (both), 92, 93 (below), 94 (both), 95, 96 (both), 100, 101, 109 (below), 116, 148 (above), 149 (below)

Paul Langrock/Zenit: pages 2/3, 11 (below), 126 (both), 127 (both), 130 (above left and below right), 135 (both), 138 (below), 139 (below), 152

Museum Checkpoint Charlie: pages 17 (above), 25 (below), 36 (below), 38, 57 (above), 64 (above), 65, 66 (right), 67, 68, 73 (above), 78 (above), 79 (above), 82 (above left and right), 85 (both), 86 (above), 87 (both), 88 (both), 93 (above), 140 (above)

Novosti Press Agency: page 21 (below)

Ali Paczensky/Zenit: pages 107 (below), 125 (above), 129, 147 (below), 156 (both), 157 (above)

Presse-Foto Röhnert, Berlin: pages 18 (above), 21 (above), 23, 23, 24, 60

Günter Schneider: pages 6, 10 (both), 11 (above), 97, 102 (both), 103 (both), 106 (both), 107 (above), 109 (above), 111 (both), 113 (above), 114 (both), 115 (below), 117 (above), 154 (below), 155 (both)

Andreas Schoelzel: pages 118 (below), 119 (both), 122 (above), 123 (both), 125 (below), 126 (above), 128 (both), 131 (above right), 136 (both), 137, 139 (above), 141 (below), 142 (both), 143 (both), 144 (both), 145, 146, 147 (above), 150, 151 (both), 154 (above)

Scigala Design, Berlin: page 89 (below)

Rolf Steinberg: pages 12, 134

Hans Peter Steibing/Zenit: pages 1, 9 (above), 98, 104, 105, 108, 110 (below), 112, 113 (below), 115 (above), 120 (below), 121 (below), 124, 126 (below), 130 (above and below right). 132, 138 (above), 149 (above), 153 (above)

US Air Force, courtesy Rolf Steinberg: pages 29, 30, 31, 34

US Army photograph: page 26